THE TRIBELESS WEST

AN OVERVIEW

SIMON LENNON

The Tribeless West: An Overview
Non-Fiction (Political Philosophy, Social Philosophy)
A book in the collection: The West
Published by Pine Hill Books
Copyright © 2020 by Simon Lennon.
ISBN 978-1-925446-38-8 (electronic)
ISBN 978-1-925446-39-5 (paperback)
61,000 words
Cover image: London, 2004

To my cousin Colin Brackpool
and in memory of his wife Marion Brackpool,
of Coulsdon, Surrey

CONTENTS

PREFACE

White people are the kindest, most generous race on earth, except with each other. We are also the most hated race on earth, primarily by ourselves.

Only we berate our forebears and disregard our descendants. We embrace diversity at our collective expense, advancing equality to our collective loss, without sense of either. We pursue inclusion of other races while excluding our own. We welcome our racial decline, even our racial suicide, as no other race does. Collectively and thus individually, we have lost our instinct to survive.

Examining how we came to this extraordinary situation and its implications is my collection of eleven non-fiction books titled *The West*, comprising four series of two or three books each: *Individualism*, *Identity*, *Nationalism*, and *Cultures*. This overview, *The Tribeless West*, collates into a single volume the principal ideas from the second series, *Identity*, comprising:

    1. *People's Identity: Race and Racism*.

    2. *Of Whom We're Born: Race and Family*.

    3. *Biological Us: Gender and Sexuality*.

People's Identity and *Of Whom We're Born* are essentially the same books. The former is a book of politics. The latter is a book of science.

A companion overview, *The Unnatural West*, collates into a single volume the principal ideas from the first series, *Individualism*. Being tribeless is unnatural.

These overviews omit the foundations, evidence, and examples supporting those ideas, for which readers so interested may turn to those eleven books and their bibliographies. Generally, those foundations, evidence, and examples are in the book described by the chapter in which those ideas appear. For ease of reading and understanding, some ideas appear in other chapters of this overview and its companion overviews.

Much as the Far East means East Asian races, their cultures, and civilisations and the Middle East means Arabs, Jews, and their cultures and civilisations, so does the West mean peoples racially European, our cultures and civilisation. Whether Europeans are one race or several races and the West is one civilisation or several civilisations, such as English, Scottish, Irish, and so forth, is a matter of nomenclature, as it is for other races and ethnicities. We could be said to be different European races but the same Western Civilisation.

Westerners are white people. People hostile to the West are hostile to white people, and vice versa. People defending one defend the other.

Please consider the ideas in this overview and the books. If the West is going to progress from this Age of Ideology to a New Age of Enlightenment, an Age of Re-Enlightenment, back to reason, morality, and the pursuit of truth, we are going to have to learn again to consider ideas new to us. We will need again to discuss matters rationally with each other.

1. PEOPLE'S IDENTITY: RACE AND RACISM

Paradoxically perhaps, any identity less than the whole of human existence lets a person feel part of a group. When two or more people share an identity, they are a tribe.

In evolutionary terms, tribes and other groups are beneficial for survival. They facilitate collecting food and water, and the provision of shelter. They help men and women find mates and care for their children. They provide protection from outsiders.

Human beings are innately wary of outsiders, because outsiders could bring disease, steal resources, or kill or hurt them. Our human instinct to survive is an instinct to live among our kind, keeping us safe.

Through primitive and historical times, natural fears protected people from dangers. People fearing outsiders were more likely to survive and procreate.

Thus over generations, humans naturally became more prejudiced against outsiders. They knew outsiders were prejudiced against them.

That is, except for white people after World War II. Scarred by the Jewish Holocaust, we lost our sense of other races being outsiders: of outsiders being outsiders.

Unwilling to feel more separate from people of other races than from people of our race, but ultimately unable to feel anything but separation from people of other races, we came also to feel separate from people of our race. Whether other people are close or far away, we slowly became single solitary selves: the tribeless West.

Tribalism keeps people wary of outsiders. Individualism leaves us wary of everyone, or it should.

We do not support or defend each other. Nobody supports or defends us. We stand or fall alone.

Other races retain their natural prejudices. They support and defend each other. They stand together. The dangers remain.

Racial and other tribal loyalty are natural. Racial disloyalty is not.

Having lost our prejudice against outsiders, natural selection suggests that the numbers of white people will diminish. We might even vanish altogether.

Losing our Identity

For millennia, our races gave us hearts, histories, and heroes. Our ethnicities made each of us someone; we knew who we were. We were peoples with cultures and futures for which to prepare.

When our identities were racial, our national identities were equally racial. The English were English, the Welsh were Welsh, and so forth. Australians, New Zealanders, and Canadians (other than Quebecois) were British. We did not cease being British for being away from our gentle green islands, God's holy isles, for a few hundred years.

We were races and nations between each other, but bracketed ourselves to be European when we encountered non-Europeans. Merged into our pan-European identity, we were white.

Americans were white. If Argentinians, Chileans, Uruguayans, and other non-indigenous Latin Americans were not Spanish, Portuguese, or other particular Europeans, they were white.

That was before the Jewish Holocaust. Increasingly defining the West since World War II has come a new word, rarely used beforehand: racism. Initially, racism meant any white person's malice or prejudice against other races. The word came quickly to mean any racial discrimination by us, however trivial. Soon enough, believing race had any practical consequences became racist. In time, any recognition by white people that races even exist became racist.

Racism is biological tribalism around race. Where nations are synonymous with races, racism is biological nationalism.

Wherever white people live in the world, we stopped identifying with our race: living or dead. We lost our identity.

Race is a collective identity. We became individuals. Our rejection of racism is Western individualism.

We are not peoples. There is nothing left to define. Our identity is not to have an identity, at least in biology.

The Primary Human Identity

Without a common identity, there is no tribalism. When we lost our ethnic and other racial identities, we lost our tribes.

No longer considering ourselves to be peoples less than all the people on earth, we consider our people to be all people; all people are one. Our sense is of a single world populace, encompassing those alien to us. We are a great global unit, a universal oneness, we push further and further to a conclusion we do not contemplate.

Proudly without a people, we identify with the world. The world does not identify with us.

Other races retain their racial roots: their racism. They have not lost their identities.

No self-respecting race would deny its identity, without a benefit in pretending. While we declare immigrants and us to be one in the same, they do not.

North Africans born in Europe call themselves the *beur* for men or *buerette* for women. Since 1992, the former has been the name of a radio station in Paris.

Their connectedness is with each other, not with Europe. If being *beur* is pejorative, it is for those who have lost something of their cultural heritage for being born in Europe.

Enjoying no end of clubs, coalitions, and countries predicated upon race, people of other races remain defined by their race without thought of being anything else. Their race is not simply their cultural heritage, as the West treats their race to be if we treat their race to be anything.

Their race is their identity. Traditional tribalism remains important to many races, but race is and will remain the primary human identity.

When we recognise other races, they are not races but communities, peoples, or cultures. We normally recognise immigrants only in abstract, without noticing the race of individuals.

That does not deter those individuals from recognising their race. They recognise each other person's race. They recognise ours.

Their identities give them histories to own and cultures to share: the comfort of race. With pride in their race, wherever they live in the world, comes honouring their ancestors, valuing their cultures, history, and traditions, and helping their descendants.

Our racial identities used to do the same. They no longer do.

While we criticise our countries and races to the world, other races keep their confidences. Criticisms they keep to themselves, while declaring only pride to everyone else.

There remains a world of races and racial loyalties indifferent to what white people think. Other races are comfortable with who and what they are. We are no longer comfortable with who and what we are.

Being white has come to mean being unable to see ourselves as other races see themselves. More and more absorbed with being individuals, race we now find confronting.

Race and Nationality

Across much of the earth, race and nationality are synonymous. They used to be for us.

If people's race and nationality are not synonymous, then race is their identity. Their race is their tribe, although they typically have more tribes within their race, most notably their families.

Race is their identifying noun. Their birthplace, citizenship, and residency are merely descriptive adjectives, when the racial noun is inadequate. They are minor points of distinction within races otherwise one in the same, distinguishing without dividing them.

Outside their races, geography does not matter. National borders can seem artificial, particularly when they are not being enforced. They do not make people into something they are not.

Countries outside the West do not deny their indigenous races their identities to accommodate immigrants or other minorities. They might have lived there for centuries, but Chinese in Malaysia are not Malays, not even Chinese Malays. If they are not simply Chinese, they are Malaysian Chinese.

Malaysian is the means of linking indigenous Malays with the indigenous people of Sabah and Sarawak. It is not a means of denying indigenous people their identities.

We used to be the same. We are not anymore.

Nationality became, to the West, infinitely more important than race; what had been the descriptive adjective became the defining noun. The West relegated race (or whatever moniker we use to mean race) to the background. Race ceased being our defining noun to become adjectival: a mere descriptor of a person, if we mention race at all.

If people are anything more particular than all the people on earth and more than mere individuals, then for the tribeless West citizenship defines them. Without race, we are simply citizens, if that.

Only in the West do immigrants take the identities of their hosts. We insist all British citizens are British.

Immigrants to Britain become British. We equate those who wage war against us with those who defend our fighting isles, and with those whose ancestors died doing so. Being British effortlessly changes from one race to another, replacing us.

Conversely, we insist only British citizens are British. Those of us who were British by our race, whose ancestors built the mother country and might have died defending her but who settled around her Empire instead of staying at home, lost our British identities. Only in the West do we deny our races our identities.

Nor are colonial Europeans really Australians, New Zealanders, or anything else anymore. Indigenous people do not think we are part of their race. We are not among their tribes.

Of all the races in which colonial Europeans take refuge since rejecting our race, no choices are more popular than our indigenous peoples. Only with indigenous people do colonial Europeans recognise the race of individuals, and not only because we base additional benefits that we give them upon it.

Indigenous people can be described by their race, without talk of nationality. That is, unless we think the extra word affirms their case to get something other citizens get, or to be something other citizens are.

We are people without nouns to define us or adjectives to describe us, which mean anything anyway, although we do not think much about it. Being white is not being anything else.

Were we instead like other races and the rest of the world, only British people would be British. Immigrants would remain what they were before they arrived, or before their parents, grandparents, or other forebears arrived.

We might grant them adjectives to distinguish them from each other, but we would not make them British. They might be British Indians, for example, but not Indian Britons and certainly not

British, any more than Britons born in India are Indian. Race makes identity easy.

Redefining Countries

In our determination to overcome race, we might still feel less than every person on earth. We might still feel our countries.

Redefining our countries to include immigrants, some Western countries have sought to redefine their countries without race. They cannot.

Being a land of liberty, equality, or fraternity is not a definition of any country. Other countries enjoy each of them too.

Hardly a country anywhere does not claim liberty, interpreting liberty as it chooses. One person's liberty is another person's constraint. One country's liberty is another country's chaos.

Equality of opportunity is at odds with equality of outcome. People are not equally clever, talented, or disciplined. We might denote people equal, but we cannot make them the same.

Fraternity presupposes something joining people together. Without race or other biology, we have no suggestion of what that could be.

In this Age of Ideology, we might imagine that countries are ideas, but countries are not ideas. Countries are countries. Many countries share the same ideas, especially around the West. The only countries uniquely holding ideas unique in the world hold ideas that we do not want for our countries.

The ideas that we do want, other countries have too. Values, idealism, and character do not define any country, just as they do not define any company or person. Any identity based upon them is vague.

Without race, the result is an ideological sense of nationhood. It becomes more words we bandy about.

For the rest of the world, race remains at the fore. Values and ideals do not enter into it. China does not treat Britons born in Hong Kong as being anything but British. Whatever values they might share, Britons will never be Chinese.

What remains without race is bureaucratic definition. To say our identity lies in our citizenship or the passport or other documentation we hold, when we offer those identities to others while enjoying our right to renounce our identity, is to say we have no identity. We have no tribe. The freedoms we had to be British and so forth, we no longer have.

When we trivialise citizenship and being left without race, our tribeless mindset becomes again that of the world, but the world is unimaginably big. Nothing less than the whole of humanity usurps us, but humanity is too many people to comprehend.

The more millions and billions of people there are in the world, the more solitary each individual becomes, but being a solitary individual becomes better than being no one at all. Ridden of everything else, we are each left alone in our mandatory isolation: individuals or everyone with no steps in between.

Racism and Individualism

Unwilling to defend our collective interests, the tribeless West defers to minorities. Minorities rule suits minorities better than it suits majorities, but becoming minorities in streets, suburbs, and whole cities have not allowed white people to enjoy our racial identities.

No amount of loyalty and belonging among other races inspires us to loyalty and belonging among our race. We still refuse to form business, cultural, sporting, or other associations around race, as people of other races do. We condemn white people who would associate with each other by race, although they would only be doing what we excuse, even endorse, people of other races doing.

People of other races continue unconcerned about racism, unless it is directed *against* their race. They like discrimination that favours their race.

Only white people oppose prejudice *by* our race. Indifferent to other races' discriminations against us, all that matters is that white people do not discriminate. We are determined not to discriminate against other races, not to be seen to discriminate, and to prevent others from our race discriminating.

We are offended not by what people of other races say about us, but what people of our race say about other races. Hungrily, we object to any hint of racism that identifies with us, likes us, or cares about us, favouring or even defending us, our histories, people, and cultures, except against other white people. We are the only race who reviles our own for being loyal to us.

In spite of their loyalty to us, we have no loyalty to white racists. Individualists have no loyalty to anyone.

When people of other races condemn racism against their race, they assert their collectivism: their connectedness with others from their race. When we condemn white people's racism, we assert our individualism: our separation from others among our race.

Nationalism, racism, and collective religion offer community and belonging. Individualism refuses community and belonging.

Our rejection of race is a rejection of commonality, community, and belonging: tribalism. We are not to identify people, befriend them, or presume anything about them by reference to anyone else, not even thousands or millions of anyone else, and not even us. Instead, we are to treat each person as a single solitary unit. It is compulsory individualism, in our perception of others and our sense of us.

There is a painful irony in feeling like a lone voice against individualism, but we remain solitary individuals if that is all we know and that is all others let us be. The individualism we assert for ourselves we demand in each other.

We love to exhort the power of one when the one defied our past racism. When the one defies our present rejection of racism, defying our demagoguery, we are merciless.

Our Tribal Anti-Tribalism

People of other races normally think about race. White people normally do not, unless there is something good to say about other races or bad to say about ours. If there is not something to say, we invent it.

No other race makes so central to its literature a fictitious story of their race mistreating someone from another race, as we do with Harper Lee's 1960 novel *To Kill a Mockingbird*. There has become no more heroic an act for a white person to perform than to fight other white people's prejudice, as does the hero in that story. It was the heroism of ending the Jewish Holocaust in 1945: our only enduring heroism, however slow it was coming.

Without racial identities, we have lost commonality with our great artists, composers, and craftsmen. Instead, our commonality is with anyone who opposed our past racism: our tribal anti-tribalism.

We gave up our past heroes and heroines for the sake of other races, but our opposition to white racism accords us new heroes and heroines, sharing our pursuit. Working against white people does not diminish our esteem for people of other races. It accentuates it.

Other races turn to their own for heroes and heroines. They make heroes and heroines from people of races not theirs when those people help their race, not when they work against it.

Loyalty to our race would be racist. Our avowed disloyalty to our race proves our opposition to racism: our cause for crusade. We flee the weakness and vulnerability of Western individualism by trying to join other races in hostility to our own.

While other races are inspired by stories of their race doing well, we are most inspired by stories of other races doing well. As much as anything else, we interpret their success as being all the greater because we think they overcame white racism. We obsess with white people's racism and presume other races are poor victims of it.

Never is our need to feel part of a tribe more palpable than in our willingness to side with other races against our own, rather than feel left alone. We are still alone.

Embracing other races unconcerned by their racism, we think people of other races are our brothers and sisters. They do not see the same of us, although they might speak as if they do when they want us to give them something or allow them something.

Their tribes are their race, at most. Our tribe is still our race, but not all our race. Refusing to embrace our race, we ostracise white racists. Our tribes are those segments of our race who also oppose our race.

Individualism falls away in our revulsion at white people's racism. We feel belonging not from being part of our race but from being part of a vengeful, cruel mob. We shout down white racists because other people do, when saying anything else would be hard. All the tribal instincts other races express through their racial identities, we express through our new-found opposition to white racism.

White racists are freaks when few of us are freaks. No one defends white racists, no one saves them. Assaulting white racists is the easy assault, the coward's assault.

Lambasting their racism lets us release contempt and hatred within us, venting emotions we dare not otherwise vent. We are the righteous lynch mobs, hanging the white man or woman we call racist from a tree.

White Identity

White people can no longer bear to think of our identity being race, but race remains at our core. Becoming disinterested in race, we have become transfixed with racism. Racism matters more to us than everything else, except race.

The West's rejection of racism, not all racism but only our racism, defines white people. It has become our identity no less surely than race used to be. It is our certainty, conviction, and existential sense of what we are.

Other races have their races. We have our opposition to racism.

It is our racial anti-racial identity, not theirs. We need other races to retain their racial identities for us to distinguish ourselves from them.

Their racial identities reside in what they are. Ours is what we oppose. Our ideals define us, but they are the ideals of what we condemn.

We remain as separate from other races as we always were, and as they remain separate from each other. Our friendships with people of other races depend upon our willingness to respect their racial loyalties, while not maintaining any of our own.

Other races are not people from whom we learn or try to understand. Instead, they have become merely a means of us demonstrating our rejection of racism. We think we like other races by not liking our own, love them by not loving our own, but we do not like them or love them as much as we reject our past racism.

The result is an ideological identity, when nothing is more important to us than ideology. Ours remains no less a racial identity than any other, except that ours is unique for bringing us no comfort or a people or place to call our own. It gives us none of the loyalties other races enjoy.

Race remains at the forefront of our thinking, but it is the race of everyone else. We are no more or less racist than people of other races and everyone is racist, but we of the West have become proudly prejudiced against our forebears, each other, and ourselves: our own.

We reject our race because we reject our racism. We respect other races because we respect their racism.

Race consumes us more in our rejection of racism than it did when we were comfortably racist. We were never so obsessed with race as we became when we turned against our race.

Jewish Identity

Our Western post-racial vision is for us. Other races do not share that vision for themselves.

The Jewish definition of being born a Jew is narrower than the Nazi definition. Jewish law insists that a person's maternal grandmother must have been Jewish for the person to be Jewish. Any Jewish grandparent made a person Jewish under the Nuremberg race laws of 1935.

For the tribeless West, the grandchild decides whether he or she is Jewish. We are not acceding to anyone's laws.

Like other immigrants, even after more than a millennium in Europe, being Jews is the noun. Their birthplaces and citizenry are, if anything, mere adjectives.

Jews normally do not consider themselves Western, except geographically, adjectivally. European Jews have identity apart from being European. British Jews are Jews, however much they might also be British.

All Jews are responsible for one another, says a Talmudic phrase. Jews also help other races, for which Arabs accuse them of courting favour, but a Jewish sense of social justice offers less help to poor Jews or poor Westerners than it does to people of other races. Proud as they are, neither rich nor poor Jews admit to there being poor Jews. Poor Westerners are more obvious.

Complaints about so-called white privilege (made often, but not only, by Jews) are frequently complaints about Jewish privilege. We generally consider Jews to be white.

Jews normally do not. Their talk of white guilt is our guilt for having committed the Holocaust, the *Shoah*.

When Jews consider themselves white, their hostility to white people becomes self-loathing. Their talk of white guilt is the guilt of having survived the Holocaust, when so many Jews did not.

As Nazis said and as Jews agree, being racially Jewish is distinct from being religiously Jewish. A Jew is racially a Jew, although Jews are the race that dares not speak its name. Jews used to speak their name, before the Holocaust.

Many Jews have come to prefer being called Jewish people rather than Jews. For the most part, to be Jewish is to practice the Jewish religion, which many Jews do not.

For our part, we speak of Jewish communities, without presuming anything of their religious beliefs. We can thus only be speaking of race, although we particularly hate ascribing race to Jews. It brings back bad memories. We might describe them as being of the Jewish faith, without regard for whether they really have faith.

Jews are a collective people. We rarely label an individual a Jew or Jewess anymore, although we are quick to call someone a Holocaust survivor or relation of Holocaust victims.

The Holocaust is the central element of Israeli identity. What is true of Israel is true of the Jews.

Hitler Jude

As well as the categories of exemptions from the Nuremberg race laws, individual Jews exempted included Erich Milch, who Nazi dictator Adolf Hitler declared an honorary Aryan. Milch was one of two Jews among the thirty or so field marshals in the armies of Nazi Germany. In those armies were thousands more Jews.

They are sometimes known as the Hitler Jews. Another group of German Jews has also been called Hitler Jews.

Many Jews in Germany lived like Germans with little thought of being Jewish until the rise of National Socialism and the Nazis coming to power in 1933. In previous centuries and in other countries, Jews had escaped discrimination by changing their religion, or at least pretending to do so. That no longer worked.

Amidst Nazi persecution, the *Hitler Jude* found their Jewish heritage, culture, and faith. They were again the chosen people of the Torah, and were punished for it. They learnt to pray in the ghettos.

When World War II embroiled Europe, anti-Semitic persecution became the Jewish Holocaust. If ever Jews were going to pray, they prayed in the death camps. Watching their hapless people die, they might well have begged the God of Moses to grant them another exodus. In the screams of others or screams of their own in their gas-chamber hell, they must have felt abandoned.

The experiences shared by disparate Jews and Jewesses who survived the Holocaust, and most of them did, haunted them, their children, and their grandchildren. No amount of killing could change their Jewish race, but it could crush their Jewish faith.

A minority of Jews remain religiously devout. The rest are racially Jews but often atheists or agnostics, if not completely indifferent to the notion of god.

Those Jews continue to feel abandoned if, at least in some inadvertent recesses of their minds, they remember they are Jewish. For the God of Moses to have abandoned their people to Nazism, then the God of Moses was not there. That god died, or never was, they feel.

Races should enjoy their cultures, but second only to white people in not enjoying their culture are the Jews. When they died, Jews (like Europeans) were traditionally buried, but Jews (like Europeans) are now often cremated. Nazis showed similar disregard for Jewish tradition by cremating corpses in the extermination camps.

There is a deep dichotomy between a profound consciousness of being racially Jewish and any feelings of pride or, for that matter, shame for being Jewish. Ambivalence is better than pain.

They are no longer *Hitler Jude*, but the legacy remains. Theirs is a post-Jewish atheism, agnosticism, or indifference shaped by the Holocaust. Post-Jewish Jewry is Jewry nevertheless.

There is nothing more natural for a race than to prevent another race from harming it. Not only could Germans commit a Holocaust, reasoned the Jews and soon enough us. Other white people could commit a Holocaust too, we potential perpetrators and recidivists, if we are not kind to other races.

Other races could commit a Holocaust too, but we do not think about them. That would be racist.

Jews living in Israel know that other races can also harm them. Jews living in the West worry more about white people.

No longer trusting god to save them, Jews strive to save themselves. Being Jewish is to do everything they can to keep white people from harming them again. Eradicating white racism, ripping away our racial gestalt, would avert another Holocaust, at least one premised upon race and one committed by us.

There is nothing more natural for a race than to exact revenge upon another race harming it, uninterested in whether that other race felt its actions were self-defence. It is all a bit incongruous for the race at the forefront of ending Western racial identities to retain racial identity for itself, but Jewish racism was not their problem. Our racism was. If there were really no race, if race were really an obsolete concept as many Jews and Westerners now claim, then there would be no Jewish race, but there defiantly is.

A hunter should never wound a lion, or it will come back and kill him. Kill it, or leave it be.

Jewish Themes

Much of the West, including Germany before 1933, generally welcomed or at least tolerated Jews. Nevertheless, we perceived arrogance and aloofness from Jews.

Especially in business and monetary matters, we perceived Jews to be greedy. Business dealings between races were more exacting than those within races.

When people understood morality in terms of tribalism, neither Jews nor we expected morality between races, moderating our dealings with each other. Separation cut both ways.

If Englishmen and women blamed Jews for Britain declaring war upon Germany in 1939, that was not a reason to cease anti-Semitism. It was more reason through the course of the war to be anti-Semitic.

However anti-Semitic many of us were, we were not harming Jews. We killed Germans, but not to save Jews. The long dark shadow of Holocaust matters more to the West in retrospect than it did at the time.

The Jewish Holocaust ended in 1945. Public revelations of the Holocaust began in 1945.

Anti-Semitism became wrong in Western eyes. It became unwarranted. It became inexcusable.

Jews object most vehemently to anti-Semitism, while recognising since the Holocaust the dangers to them that any white people's prejudice can be. Among Hollywood and other creative forces, condemning racial and religious prejudice became a Jewish theme.

Through countless films, television programmes, books, and news media, Jews reduced race to skin colour and eye shape. They claimed people were born without racism. They preached racial integration, for the West. They demonised white racial discrimination: any differentiation by race.

Black and other non-white characters became genii, heroes, and victims. White characters became fools, cowards, and villains, with racist white characters the worst. Ironically, Jewish actors and actresses often played racist white people, even Nazis, in films and television programmes. Other white characters could be complicit in their racism, if they failed to refute it.

A slander against Jews would be anti-Semitism. There is no word for slanders against white people. We committed the Holocaust. This was justified prejudice, warranted by the Jewish Holocaust as other prejudice was not, although we thought anti-Semitism was justified before the Holocaust.

With enough repetition, Western audiences could hardly help but agree. So increasingly did white writers, film-makers, and others. Jewish themes became our themes.

While we dwell upon our past attitudes to Jews, we ignore Jewish attitudes to us. To many Jews, we have traditionally been and remain *goyim*, or simply *goy*: amoral non-Jews, who Jews cannot trust. If *goy* is not necessarily derogatory in other contexts, then *sheigetz, shiksa*, and *shvartza* are, even if Jews do not use those Ashkenazic words in our presence.

Different races naturally mistrust each other. Jews do not trust us. Before the Holocaust, we did not trust Jews. Morality is tribal.

Almost a century after the Holocaust, Jews have no greater friend on earth than the West, but cannot see it. Muslim anti-Semitism does not diminish Jews' particular wariness of white people for perpetrating the Holocaust. We are Israel's best bastion beside its people, but remain a risk in Jewish eyes: an existential threat.

Like white people (although not so much people of other races), Jews are not all of one mind. More so than white people, most Jews are.

Meanwhile, fewer and fewer Jews own their ancient cultural heritage. More damaging than persecution is tolerance.

German Identity

The Germans' long tolerance of Jews made Jews numerous in Germany by the time of the Great War. The war that shattered Europe shattered that tolerance too.

From the Great War came Soviet communism. In response to either the Great War or Soviet communism, or both, came Nazism. From Nazism came the Holocaust.

Not only Jews died in the Holocaust. So did Germany.

Germany again welcomes Jews, but much as the Holocaust redefined Jews, it redefined Germans. Erasing centuries of German cultural, intellectual, and scientific achievements, the Holocaust became Germany's only history.

Instead of keeping their past misdeeds to the peripheries or concealing their misdeeds altogether as other races do, Germans and Austrians build monuments to their Holocaust victims in towns and cities across their countries. They keep finding new categories of victims of Nazism and long-dead Germans at war, but Germans do not recognise themselves among those victims. Defying every instinct to survive, Germans do not care if their race disappears.

Wars are not the problem. The Holocaust is.

Unconcerned by the crimes of other races, Germans stand not merely convicted of their racial guilt, but consumed by it. Relentlessly, they punish themselves.

In our fight against our white racist past, we have no greater force than tribeless Germany. Germans are at odds with their parents and grandparents. Veterans are at odds with themselves. It is their war of liberation against a totalitarian dictatorship, but one in which Germans have taken responsibility as no other race on earth takes for its dictators. It is their chance to join the rest of the

West against a common foe: that moment in history when their race traditionally among the most tolerant of Jews was never more intolerant.

To this day, people knowing only one aspect of World War II know that Germany murdered six million Jews. Exact casualty figures are often unknowable, but suggestions of a lower casualty figure should console us. Instead, they offend us so determined to think the worst of white people.

We know nothing else about Nazis, their policies, or actions. We do not wonder why they killed Jews. We are not conscious that something like sixty million other people also died through World War II. As many as eleven million Russians, Poles, Yugoslavs, and others, including Germans, also died in the Holocaust.

Victim Germans

Everybody lost World War II. Germany lost most. A similar number of Germans as Jews died in the war. They amounted to more than ten percent of the German population.

Germany does not become a victim race. We feel no guilt or inflict condemnation about British and American bombers killing something like forty thousand German civilians in February 1945 while destroying the cultural city of Dresden, with little or no military significance.

We are fixated with the wrongs that Westerners committed against other races. We are not so interested about wrongs that we committed against each other, and still commit.

For all our apologies to Jews, we do not apologise to Germans for the massive land seizures and cruel reparations that the victorious powers (especially France) imposed upon Germany in the 1919 Treaty of Versailles. Long before the Nazis came to power, Winston Churchill recognised in 1924 that German bitterness towards France risked another war. In all our contemplations that other races' misconduct might be due to our past misdeeds, we do not contemplate France's role in humiliating Germany after the Great War for the rise of Nazism.

Paradoxically, Adolf Hitler's rebuilding of Germany through the 1930s could have diminished that risk of war, even if German bitterness towards France remained. In 1939, Germany invaded the

Polish Corridor dividing Germany from Danzig to bring those Germanic lands back within Germany. Hitler might have ordered the consumption of Czechoslovakia before the invasion of the Polish Corridor because he knew Germany's claim to the Polish Corridor was much stronger than any claim to Czechoslovakia beyond the Sudetenland.

Nor do we apologise for Germany's land forfeitures and other suffering immediately after World War II. Germans had enslaved people of other races to labour during World War II. Afterwards, France enslaved several hundred thousand German prisoners of war to labour in France. Forced labour of Germans continued into the 1950s.

At the Potsdam Conference early in 1945, America, Britain, and the Soviet Union agreed that Czechoslovakia could expel all ethnic Germans after the war. Czechoslovakia did.

The evictions were not political. They were racial. Those sorrowed and frightened German men, women, and children were evicted from the Sudetenland without thought as to who were Nazis. They were evicted for being German, lost among the guilty people.

The only apologies we do not make are to white people. We do not warrant our apology.

The Nuremberg trials did not allow individual Germans to defend the charges against them on the grounds that they were simply following orders under threat of death. We expected them to have died rather than kill Jews.

We still do. So, now, do Germans.

Following the Holocaust came an era of revenge against Germany. The war was not over.

The threat from the communist Soviet Union led to the Marshall Plan benefiting West Germany, but the Plan benefited countries throughout Western Europe. It was an economic measure, while Germany's punishments persisted.

Of all the suffering in the world of which we hear so much, the suffering of which we hear the least has been Europe's. The least of the least has been Germany's. No people in history have been punished as Germans have been punished for the Holocaust.

Good Germans

John Rabe was deputy group leader of the Nazi Party in Nanjing in 1937, when the Imperial Japanese Army entered the city. Rabe and other Westerners created the Nanking Safety Zone in all the foreign embassies and at Nanjing University, saving at least two hundred and fifty thousand Chinese from massacre by Japanese. Rabe also housed six hundred and fifty Chinese safely in his properties.

Rabe wrote to Nazi German dictator Adolf Hitler that *"there is a question of morality here… I cannot bring myself for now to betray the trust these people have put in me, and it is touching to see how they believe in me."*

At its peak, no more than ten percent of Germans were members of the Nazi Party, doubtlessly including many joining for the sake of their careers in a totalitarian state. They were not the same ten percent of Germans who died during World War II.

We presume all Germans participated in the Holocaust, but only a tiny proportion did. Many Jews survived the Holocaust because networks of Germans risked their lives to save them.

Most Nazi Party members did not participate in the Holocaust. Nazi Party member Oskar Schindler famously saved a thousand Jews.

At the Auschwitz concentration camp, at least some German guards were kind, especially to children. They acknowledged the craziness they could not stop.

Germans treated British and other soldiers and prisoners of war according to the Geneva Conventions. Throughout their occupation of Paris, Germans allowed French Great War veterans to continue lighting a flame above France's Tomb of the Unknown Soldier at six thirty each night.

Hitler ordered German soldiers to respect all war memorials, including those of his enemies. The only war memorial the Nazis destroyed was one portraying a German soldier being killed in the Great War.

Two German soldiers caught urinating on a British war memorial were offered the choice between committing suicide and serving on the Russian Front. They chose the latter.

In September 1942, a German U-boat fired upon and sank the Royal Mail Ship *Laconia*, believing her to be carrying British troops, but the sight and cries of drowning passengers told Captain Werner

Hartenstein otherwise. He began rescuing Italian prisoners of war, Polish guards, and British women and children under the Red Cross flag, while other German U-boats came to assist. They saved hundreds of Italian, Polish, and British lives before an American B-24 Liberator bombed them. Of necessity, Admiral Karl Dönitz subsequently ordered German submarines not to attempt rescuing survivors from downed ships.

Field Marshal Erwin Rommel defied Hitler's orders to kill captured Jewish soldiers. He was implicated in a plot to kill Hitler in 1944, costing Rommel his life.

Rommel's counterpart George Patton was arguably the most aggressive and combative American general in war, proudly taking more German casualties than any other general. Upon Germany's surrender, Patton stopped fighting. Revelations of the Holocaust did not dissuade him from the view that Germans were decent people, possibly the most decent in Europe. Leaving Nazis in office, he equated the political conflicts between Nazis and others to those between America's principal political parties.

None of it matters to Germans any more than it matters to Jews. Germany's remorse to the Jews did not have to affect her relations with other races, but she responded to the Holocaust not just in her treatment of Jews but in her treatment of herself. If the Holocaust made Jewish identity fundamentally one of being a victim determined never to be a victim again, then it led to a German identity of being a criminal unable to be anything else. If Germans are not to be goose-stepping, genocidal racists, then they had better be diehard opponents of their race, they feel.

Genocidal Turkey

Rejecting our past racism, Britons have come to mourn enemies past, other than Nazis, as the equals of our soldiers. Among them are the Turks.

The Turks are an Asian race. Seizing its opportunity, the Ottoman Empire joined the Great War on Germany's side in November 1914, when Germany seemed she could win. The Ottoman Empire was not European. It was Asian, encroaching upon European soil.

Three million soldiers fought for the Ottoman Empire in the Great War alone, but we make representative of all Turkish soldiers a single Turkish soldier waving a white flag to help a wounded British soldier in the first Anzac campaign, 1915. It is our new-found conviction that their soldiers were as noble as ours, if not nobler. Anything else would be racist.

In 1915, a fifth of Turkey's population was Christian. That single good soldier might also have been Christian.

Our fixation with that single good Turk belies the fact that the day before that first Anzac Day, the twenty-fifth of April 1915, Muslim Turks began their massacre of two million Christian Armenians. Turks did not value life as we did.

Turks feel no shame for the atrocities of their racial past as we feel for ours. Turks are proud of being Turks. Under pressure from Turkey, the American Congress deferred for decades consideration of an Armenian Genocide Resolution finally introduced in 2007.

The Turkish Penal Code prohibited insulting *"Turkishness"* until 2008, since which time it has prohibited insulting *"the Turkish Nation."* Both provisions forbid talk of the Armenian Genocide. Turks acknowledge only that some Armenians were deported or starved, or that criminal acts by Armenian gangs necessitated Turks killing them.

Turkey prohibits people from saying the Armenian Holocaust occurred. Conversely, Germany, Austria, and other European countries prohibit people from saying the Jewish Holocaust did not occur, or supposedly trivialising it by questioning the number of Jews killed.

Guilt-laden post-Holocaust Germany goes so far as to bring responsibility upon herself for the Armenian Genocide. Her rationale is Germany having been Ottoman Turkey's ally in the Great War.

Defending their racial reputation, foreign citizenship does not keep Turks from being Turks of the Turkish Nation. Wherever they live in the world, Turks demand that other races not mention their massacres, of which there were several.

During and after the Great War, Turks also massacred hundreds of thousands of Christian Assyrians, almost erasing the Assyrians altogether. Assyrian immigrant pressure in Australia meant Turkish immigrants had little choice but eventually to accept a memorial in 2010 alluding to the Assyrian Genocide, on condition that it not mention that Turks were responsible. It would be like remembering victims of the Jewish Holocaust without mentioning Nazis.

Turkey's third genocide at the time was the Greek Genocide. From 1913 until 1923, Turks murdered as many as nine hundred thousand Greeks and destroyed much of the West's Christian and classic European heritage. On the fourteenth of November 1914, the Caliph of the Ottoman Empire declared a Holy War against infidels: Christians.

The Great War that ruined Europe might have broken up the Ottoman Empire, but it did not break the Turks as it broke Europeans. It gave rise to modern Turkey.

Exonerating Turkey

While we erupt into frenzies at the wrongs white people committed against people of other races, or allegedly committed, we are uninterested in their crimes against us. Turks were never punished for their three Christian Holocausts.

Among the punishments inflicted because of the Jewish Holocaust upon their portions of a partitioned Germany after World War II, the American, British, and French occupying forces imposed laws compelling West Germany to accept immigrants from other races. The new Federal Republic of Germany was open not just to Jews, but to everyone.

There was no pretence then that racial diversity would make Germany strong. We came up with that lie half a century later, after other Western countries opened our borders to all comers too.

The most numerous immigrants coming to Germany were the Turks, but the guilt dogging Germans is not one they besmirch upon their innocent immigrants. The tribeless West deems those immigrants to be German by their residency if not their citizenship when it is reason to give them something, even the country, but not in matters of guilt. Their race exonerates them.

Confident in themselves and in their culture, Turks retain privilege in their country, Turkey, in spite of the massacres they committed. Contemptuous of themselves and their culture, Germans grant Turks privilege in Germany, because of the massacre Germany committed, not of Turks but of Jews.

German guilt is strictly racial. In their hatred of Hitler and vengeful self-derision, Germans came to celebrate immigrants replacing their race.

Through it all, the Jewish Holocaust retains a special status. Not just the archetypal genocide it is, for Jews and the West, the only genocide: the best known killing in history.

The Armenian and other Christian holocausts committed by Turks do not recur through Jewish and Western films, television, and books as does the Jewish Holocaust. There is no revulsion against Turks, Asians, or Muslims generally as the Jewish Holocaust has created against Germans, Europeans, and Christians generally. We do not make Turkish perpetrators of genocide representative of Turks, Asians, or Muslims everywhere, then or now, as we make German perpetrators representative of Germans and the West then, now, and always.

Imperial Japan

World War II was an Asian war before it became a world war. Imperial Japan occupied Manchuria from 1931, invaded the rest of China in 1937, and thereafter expanded across Asia and the Pacific towards Australia.

Estimates vary widely, but Japanese murdered many millions, possibly tens of millions, of civilians and prisoners of war from other races from 1931 to 1945. During the Rape of Nanking, Japanese soldiers raped and murdered three hundred thousand Chinese civilians and unarmed soldiers through six weeks in 1937.

War is horrible. For Westerners, the most terrible horrors through World War II did not come from Germany but from Japan. Ours were European conventions of compassion and respect, not shared by the Japanese.

Japan did not abide by the Geneva Conventions of War. It committed numerous war crimes by Western standards, including specifically targeting marked medics. There is no common humanity.

Army surgeon Shiro Ishii and his secret Unit 731 experimented upon as many as twelve thousand non-Japanese, including Western prisoners of war. They vivisected young women in the Philippines to teach soldiers about female anatomy and infected prisoners with diseases such as syphilis. Unit 731 studied living people freezing in extreme cold and crumpling under extreme pressure. A six-foot-tall white man was cut into two and preserved in a large vial of formaldehyde.

Japanese soldiers enslaved something like two hundred thousand white and other non-Japanese women, beating and raping them as they willed. When we make a rare mention of that enslavement, we dehumanise the women. We call them the "comfort women," a delightfully inoffensive phrase making them sound like fluffy cushions on a sofa rather than sex slaves tied to Japanese beds.

When Hong Kong fell to the advancing Japanese, the Japanese slaughtered British medical staff. Twenty-one Australian Army nurses reached Bangka Island after their ship was bombed and sunk, only to be massacred by Japanese.

Instead of eating their rice, Japanese soldiers in New Guinea killed and ate Australian soldiers. Less forgiving then than the West has become, Australian soldiers in New Guinea responded by not taking Japanese prisoners of war.

Japanese captors forced their prisoners of war into slave labour, giving them little, if any, food or medical attention. Of twelve thousand American prisoners of war enslaved to work for the Japanese government and Japanese companies during the war, eleven hundred died.

In 1942, Japanese soldiers set upwards of sixty thousand Filipino and American prisoners of war on the Bataan Death March. As many as ten thousand Filipinos and six hundred and fifty Americans died.

In 1943, Japan sank the Australian hospital ship *Centaur*. Two hundred and sixty medical personnel and civilian crew died.

Japan ordered that no captured soldier should survive the war. As well as the infamous Burma Railway, the Japanese forced prisoners of war and slave labourers to build a military airstrip at Sandakan, Borneo. Most Australian and British prisoners of war and Indonesian slave labourers were already dead by early 1945, when nearby Allied landings led the camp commandant to march the last prisoners to another camp, a hundred and sixty miles away. Eighteen hundred Australian and seven hundred and thirty-eight British prisoners of war died in the Sandakan Death March. The only survivors were six prisoners who escaped.

Losing the war did not humble Japan as it humbled Germany. The Japanese reputedly sent prostitutes carrying venereal disease to meet American soldiers occupying Japan.

Rather than becoming frightened of their racism and nationalism as we became frightened of ours, war led Asians to value their races and countries more. Asian victims, especially Chinese, periodically complain that official Japanese school textbooks gloss over Japan's wartime record.

The only white people complaining that the Japanese failed to recognise their history were our returned servicemen, who had suffered and known the men and women who suffered at Japanese hands, but we dismissed our old soldiers' bigotries. They have since died.

Exonerating Japan

While Jews spoke so much about the Holocaust, our traumatised soldiers trying to come home from the war said little about Japan. The victorious Allies tried individual Japanese, but post-war pragmatism in our new alliance with Japan saved its wartime emperor Hirohito. The Japanese people were not punished as Germans were punished with immigration, enslavement, or anything else.

We forgave. Among the dead in the Sandakan Death March was Ted Dunhill. A generation or two onward, the Dunhill family of Boonderoo donated limestone rocks for the Japanese Garden in the New South Wales town of Cowra. The town came to make heroes of the Japanese who tried to escape their prisoner-of-war camp in 1944, in spite of them killing five Australians. The story of an Australian veteran befriending a former Japanese soldier was meant to inspire us further to embrace our past enemy Japan, as we do not embrace Germany.

We forgot. What once were facts we all knew, or at least some of us knew, became yesterday's secrets.

Our forebears were other people; we are not interested in other people's wars. War in Asia is yesterday's news, wars against other countries anachronistic. We do not fight other races. That would be racist.

Japan does not talk about its wartime crimes. Neither do we.

The truth being politically unacceptable, where history classes necessitate us touching upon the Asian and Pacific theatre of war, we insist there was fault on both sides: that we committed atrocities against the Japanese and the Japanese committed them against us. It is not true.

No such qualification ever accompanies criticisms of white people. No statement about the Holocaust accuses the Jews of also committing genocide against Germans.

Claiming there was fault on both sides through the war that Japan cruelly waged insults our forebears who fought, suffered, and died in our defence. We do not appreciate our forebears' sacrifice. They were racists.

The long litany of Japanese atrocities during World War II has not caused revulsion at East Asian or Japanese racism the way the Jewish Holocaust caused our obsessive revulsion at white racism. The Japanese were no less convinced of their racial superiority than we were convinced of ours, but the Jewish Holocaust made it untenable for us to impose racial guilt upon other races. Hollywood does not screen Japanese villains, except for the few films directly concerning the Asian and Pacific theatre of war. Jews and we carefully avoid perpetuating negative Japanese and other Asian stereotypes, while making them freely about white people.

We know the Japanese not by their aggression and cruelty, but their sacrifice and suffering. The most heroic Western soldier laying down his life for God and Country did not die without needing to die, but the Kamikaze pilots saw glory in suicide.

We have made Japan a victim race, as we have not made Germany. We even feel pangs of guilt because America dropped atom bombs on Hiroshima and Nagasaki forcing the Japanese surrender. Japan has never felt guilt for anything it did. Most races do not.

At our worst, we condemn our forebears for winning a war that we do not condemn Japan for starting or fighting as it did. Fearing more bombs, Japan's quick surrender following those two atomic bombs saved Western, Chinese, and other lives too, including the Japanese who would have died while the war continued.

Like others outside the West, Asians remain racist, confident in their race and cultures. None remain more certain of their biological and cultural superiority than Chinese and Japanese.

While we torment Germans, and Germans torment themselves, for the Holocaust, young Japanese remain ignorant of the slaughters and carnage their race wreaked. We do not mind.

They think they would have won their glorious adventure driving Europeans from Asia but for the two American atomic bombs, although the Americans had already taken Iwo Jima before the bombs were dropped. Japan was retreating.

Relative Horrors

We never ceased being conscious of race. Since the Holocaust, we have simply become selective about when we think of it.

Crimes by other races no longer bother us; that would be racist. Crimes by dead Europeans consume us.

Atrocities are not measured by statistics, in a leader board high in the stands. We speak of equating one life with another, one death with another, but the real measures of relative horrors are not just the numbers of victims. They are the race of the victims.

Jews suffered much more under Nazism than under communism. East Europeans suffered much more under communism than Nazism. Eastern Europeans thus dwell upon the Jewish Holocaust much less than other European peoples do, but Jews allow them no excuse. While East Europeans equate the two totalitarianisms, if only to be generous to Jews, Jews insist that Nazism was infinitely worse. Ultimately, the only basis for their claim was that Nazism targeted Jews.

White fears of being labelled racist shut down criticism and honest commentary about other races and their histories. However little the West cares about history when white people were victims, we are positively hostile to history when the people killing us were not.

Were other races' atrocities against us repeated in documentaries, entertainment, and schoolrooms with the vigour that we hear of our past failings, real and contrived, then we would hate Turks, Japanese, and other races for their crimes, most profoundly against us. With a constant repetition of the pains brought upon people by ideologies, we would hate ideologies. If all those stupid, awful white racists in films and television shows had been socialists, we would hate socialists. If we could join mobs hounding down communists, then we would hate communists for killing Ukrainians with famine. If the people we could so freely hate were Jews, we would hate Jews.

We hate none of those people. Holding only white people accountable, we hate only us.

Nothing taints other races like that staining Europeans. Other races shine in our eyes so much as to blind us, while our race burns in our brains.

Racial Guilt

Among the scientists performing experiments upon gypsies at the Auschwitz-Birkenau concentration camp was paediatrician Berthold Epstein. A Czechoslovakian Jew, Epstein's family died in Auschwitz.

We thus excused him for those experiments, as we did not excuse Germans at the Nuremberg trials who had acted under threat of death. We allow other people's race to excuse them from crimes for which they would otherwise be guilty.

Conversely, we allow our race to make us guilty of crimes of which we would otherwise be innocent. Individualism does not excuse white people from guilt that racial links impose.

We do not just deem our forebears to have been wrong. We make them representative of us. They and the peoples we say they mistreated are normally long dead, but theirs was no individual guilt. It is our racial guilt: our racial culpability.

Ours is a selective individualism. We do not treat wrongs against people of our race, even thousands or millions of people of our race, as being wrongs against our race. Identifying with victims of crime or genocide because we are of the same race would be racist.

Conversely, identifying with wrongdoers of our race we do freely, and not only as regards the Holocaust. We treat wrongdoings against people of another race, even individuals among other races, as being wrongs by our race against theirs.

Jews feel forbidden from forgetting the Holocaust. So do we.

Other European races embraced German guilt for the Holocaust as our own. The crime we made Germany's in the aftermath of the war became our crime, too. Germany's racial guilt became white racial guilt.

However white people identify ourselves in other contexts, when it comes to our inherited guilt, we are not Jews, gypsies, or other immigrants. The only people we are not are victims.

Any relationship between races has to be racial. We recognise race every time we feel ashamed for what our people did, or we are told our people did, to people of other races.

Our histories are racial: racial crimes transcending successive generations. We dwell in our racial identities, especially our racial histories, when it is a chance to punish ourselves for our race. We are not so tribeless after all.

We even hold each other, or ourselves, accountable for other races' bad deeds and ills when there is any means for us to do so. We try to find white provocation or vicarious racial guilt for any other race's crime on earth.

When people of other races do wrong, we treat their guilt as individual guilt. We dismiss the guilty of other races as small proportions of their race as we do not dismiss the guilty from among our race. We do not make governments and companies outside the West representative of their innocent races, as we make Western governments and corporations representative of us.

If the implication of people from other races doing wrong is wider than the individuals responsible, then those other races' wrongdoings blight the whole human species. The phrase "Man's inhumanity to man" is a means by which the West takes collective responsibility for wrongdoings by people of other races. We hate ourselves a little more.

The phrase "Man's inhumanity to man" is not applied to Western wrongdoings. Our failings are ours alone.

Racial Pride

We have come to believe that any mention of wrong by other races is an accusation that they do only wrong. We thus do not mention their wrongs at all. The result is a sense that they do only good.

Conversely any mention of good among white people is treated as a claim of white supremacy. We thus do not mention our good at all. The result is a sense that we do only wrong.

Our guilt is racial, pride is not. We accord collective guilt for the wrongdoings of our race damned forever, but never collective pride for the good things our race did and do. We are denied the chance to identify with our forebears or rest of our race when identifying with them and their achievements would bring us comfort, support, or companionship.

The racism we condemn is not just prejudice. It is feeling at all good about us.

We are again tribeless. Never allowing ourselves pride in our people and being of European heritage, we describe white people as if we are not. Unwilling to link ourselves with our ancestors for the good that they did, we are not free to cherish our achievements.

For the goodness we do and our forebears have done, we espouse the goodness of a mystical human spirit. We give credit for our kind deeds to all humanity, however rare those deeds are in the world, if not altogether unique to white people.

The end of Western racism and nationalism means all those reasons we once had for feeling good about us became reasons to feel good about everyone else. They do not need to be good, if we are.

On the other hand, when individuals from other races do good deeds, we treat them as representative of their races. We do not treat them as representing humanity as we treat the wrongdoers from their races. Other races' virtues we regard as their races' alone. We have more reason to like them.

Those other races agree. Proud of their people, they enjoy self-confidence, even arrogance, we lack.

We lambast arrogant white people, but never arrogance in other races. White people can be self-confident, but only for our individual selves. It is arrogance reserved in spite of our race, denied to others of our race.

At our most generous, we are supposed to think that all people on earth are equally good. At our most self-contemptuous, we are still worse than anyone else. We steadfastly refuse to love ourselves.

The Politicisation of History

History is defined by the victors. We lost.

The only purpose of history, like the only purpose of everything else in our ideological West, is political, as the Marxists decreed. Ideologues politicise the past and present into political devices, presuming they already are, with no greater political objective than eradicating white racism.

The Jewish Holocaust gave rise to a narrative that Christian Western prejudice drove oppression and war through history. The suffering of Jews through the Holocaust became the suffering of non-Europeans forever.

The narrative is untrue. Throughout history, tribes have attacked other tribes. Races have exploited other races. Races exploited their own.

We blame ourselves for the Holocaust. We do not give ourselves credit for ending it.

The history we hear and that our children are taught in school is a revision that began to appear after World War II, most obviously from the 1960s. To shame us out of our racism and delegitimise our nationalism, historians espouse a falsified history of Western foolishness and oppression, along with other races' brilliance and victimhood. They misrepresent the past to vilify our forebears and vindicate other races, editing history to exonerate everyone else.

We might dismiss failings by other races for being a long time ago. We do not dismiss failings by our race for being a long time ago.

Politics prevails, and not just with history. Alone among the races of the world, the themes of Western histories have become how awful we are.

If we are racists, then we are most complicit in white people's wickedness, almost always imagined rather than real. If we are against white people's racism, we are absolving ourselves a little from racial infamy.

With white people so keen to abuse our lesser selves, we invite other races to abuse us too. Neither they nor we tolerate our failings, real or contrived. Quietly, privately, the more thoughtful among them do not understand why we do.

When people of other races manufacture and conceal history, it is to promote their race and denigrate others, including us. The themes of their histories are how good, great, and clever they are.

We agree. They are the glorious others. Instead of our children seeing images of great Western scientists, soldiers, and statesmen, we deluge them with images of supposedly notable figures from other races. We promote races and cultures not ours.

Our rewritten history hides the history that no longer suits. Being factual is not enough to make events part of our history that suggest something good in our forebears.

Our forebears' legacy is all that remains for them to suffer. They might have lived and died long before the Holocaust, but tarnishing their legacy is their punishment for our racial guilt for the Holocaust.

Conversely, mere allegations make events parts of our history if they affirm how awful we are certain we were. We are determined to convict us all of past crimes, refusing us doubt, whatever the lack of evidence those crimes occurred or that Europeans were responsible. There is no burden of proof for alleging tales of oppression by white people inflicted upon innocent others. We need only our convictions they must have occurred because our forebears were wicked.

Denigrating Europeans is fine. Applauding us is not.

Applauding other races is fine. Denigrating them is not.

Facts are unimportant. Our thoughts about race have been emotive, not factual, since the Holocaust.

Pursuing the facts has become racist, whenever the facts were of our forebears not being as evil or stupid as we insist they were. Horrible white people are a theme of our history, and we are not willing to lose it. Other races concur.

Black Slavery

Convulsed with the sense that we are the worst of all races, our principal postmodern shame remains the Atlantic slave trade centuries ago, but slavery has been commonplace around the world throughout history. Europeans did not invent slavery. Nor have we been the race most involved in it, but rather than imagine we have no greater guilt for slavery than other races, we allow the guilt to be ours alone.

In many cases, the initial enslavement of Africans into the Atlantic slave trade was not by Europeans. It was by fellow Africans wanting to trade. Africans, Arabs, Jews, and others participated in the Atlantic slave trade, along with Europeans and Americans. African former slaves traded slaves.

Our concern is not the mandatory migration: Africans being transported against their will from one continent to another. Britain transported involuntarily to America an estimated fifty thousand convicts, almost all of whom were British or Irish. After American independence, Britain transported a further hundred and sixty-five thousand convicts to Australia, the last of whom arrived in 1868. All but a thousand or so of them were European.

They too had little choice in their journeys, but we do not worry about them. Our emancipation of other races no longer extends to our own.

The Industrial Revolution was central to the West's growing wealth, but African slaves lacked the skills, dexterity, and temperament for factories. They worked on farms where the labour was menial. While individual traders and plantation owners profited from slavery, poor Europeans lost for being denied jobs and income.

Much like other immigration, the overall monetary contribution to the West from black slavery was less than the sugar sweetening rich people's tea. Bringing home tobacco from the Americas proved harmful.

The British Empire would continue improving for another eighty years after the abolition of slavery in 1833. The biggest problem was wondering what to do with the freed.

With hindsight, we ought to have repatriated the freed slaves to Africa. During the nineteenth century, Australia conscripted Melanesian Kanaks from New Caledonia to work for food, lodging, and low wages in Pacific Rim countries and colonies, including the sugar cane plantations of Queensland. When their labour ceased, Australia repatriated them to New Caledonia. Soon enough, it no longer mattered.

In spite of millions of Africans freely and voluntarily entering the West, Africans continue to complain they suffer from white prejudice. Repatriation to Africa is still an option.

White Slavery

The modern word "slavery" comes from the same Greek word as "Slav" after Vikings captured and enslaved so many Central and East Europeans. Viking invaders of northern England took Saxon homes and enslaved my ancestors, too.

While the African slave trade to the Americas was getting under way, Italian merchants were transporting Bulgarian and other slaves to satisfy North African traders. Muslim Istanbul imported as many as two and a half million European slaves from 1450 until 1700.

From the sixteenth century, North Africans snatched more than a million European slaves in raids on coastal towns in England, Italy, France, Spain, Portugal, the Netherlands, and Iceland. They traded those slaves in markets along the Barbary Coast of North Africa, including what are now Morocco, Algeria, Tunisia, and western Libya.

Conquest by France ended the white slave trade in 1830. French imperialism saved us.

Modern definitions of slavery include indentured service, but we are not as quick to bring our forebears within that definition as we bring other races today. Most indentured servants and slaves in Britain's colonies through the seventeenth century were Irish, including many kidnapped from Ireland. During the 1650s, Britain took a hundred thousand Irish children aged from ten to fourteen years old from their parents and sold them as slaves in Virginia, New England, and the West Indies.

In 1846, black American abolitionist Frederick Douglass, a former slave, wrote that no race on earth had been more relentlessly persecuted and oppressed on account of its race and religion than the Irish. Conversely, in ancient times, Irish slave traders enslaved many English, bringing them to Ireland. Racial and religious discrimination throughout history have been complex, as our simplistic narratives cannot see.

The distinction between slavery and indentured service could be technical. What mattered most to the people concerned was how well they were treated. Many cheap Irish were treated worse than more expensive Africans were treated. Property rights made African slaves valuable, as Irish indentured servants were not.

(The Roman Catholic Irish experience of English racial and religious prejudice might have made them particularly hostile to other Western prejudice, after World War II. The Jewish experience of the Holocaust did.)

Cruel corruption of history it might be, but we damn descendants of white slaves for the crime of slavery. We honour as victims the descendants of African and Arab enslavers, slave traders, and slave keepers.

Ending Slavery

Slavery in Africa preceded Western involvement. It continued afterwards. Men of Empire like Major-General Charles Gordon did much to end slave trading and liberate oppressed people in Africa, as well as end civil war in China.

We blame ourselves for having participated in slavery. We do not give ourselves credit for ending it.

Britain abolished slavery with the Slavery Abolition Act of 1833. We emancipated all slaves across the British Empire in 1834.

Essentially buying the slaves' freedom, the Slave Compensation Act of 1837 compensated slave owners at a cost of forty percent of Britain's national budget and five percent of our gross domestic product. The British people shared the cost of abolishing slavery, as we were morally and often legally bound to do whenever governments confiscated private property for the public good, which abolishing slavery effectively did. The debt due to having abolished slavery burdened Britain thereafter.

Britain had previously abolished the slave trade in 1807, banning British ships from transporting slaves. In 1808, the Royal Navy established the West Africa Squadron to enforce the ban. Britain went onto enact treaties with other countries empowering the Royal Navy to intercept their ships to free slaves.

Africans resisted British efforts to end slavery. On a diplomatic mission to West Africa in July 1850, Captain Frederick Forbes of H.M.S. *Bonetta* failed to persuade King Ghezo to end the kingdom of Dahomey's participation in the Atlantic slave trade. "The slave trade has been the ruling principle of my people," Ghezo answered him. "It is the source of their glory and wealth. Their songs celebrate their victories and the mother lulls the child to sleep with notes of triumph over an enemy reduced to slavery."

Among the African lives saved by the British Empire was an Egbado princess Aina, born in 1843, who was orphaned at age five due to intertribal warfare. Intended for sacrifice, she had been a slave for two years when, amidst their customary exchange of gifts, King Ghezo gave her to Forbes.

Forbes renamed the girl Sara Forbes Bonetta and took her to England to raise her. Queen Victoria treated her as a goddaughter, calling her Sally. Her Majesty arranged for Sara to receive a middle-class British upbringing.

For Sara's health, she returned aged eight to Africa, where schools established by the Church Missionary Society in Freetown, Sierra Leone educated her. Aged twelve, she returned to Britain, where Reverend Frederick Scheon and his wife cared for her at their home in Gillingham. In 1862, Queen Victoria invited her to the wedding of Her Majesty's daughter Princess Alice.

The West Africa Squadron operated from 1808 until 1870. From 1808 until 1860, the Royal Navy intercepted sixteen hundred slave ships, freeing more than a hundred and fifty thousand African slaves. Among those ships, H.M.S. *Primrose* in 1830 captured the twenty-gun Cuban slave ship *Veloz Passagera*, carrying five hundred and fifty-six African slaves. Three Britons died and twelve were wounded to free those slaves.

From 1808 until 1870, two thousand Royal Navy sailors died freeing African slaves. Africans murdered them.

Among the slaves sent to the Americas from West Africa were many Akans, whose Ashanti Empire lasted from 1670 to 1957, under British occupation from 1900. The main objectives for the British expeditionary forces during the Anglo-Ashanti wars concluding in 1900 were ending slavery and the human sacrifices for which the Kings of Ashanti enslaved their fellow Africans, as well as bringing peace and security for neighbouring tribes. Tribes such as the Fante and the Ga relied upon British protection from Ashanti incursions.

Slavery does not require trade. Nor does it require Western buyers.

No race has done more through history to end slavery than we have done. No race does more now. White people have been and remain the world's most ardent opponents of slavery, wherever it happens.

The American Civil War

American Indians enslaved each other before the coming of Europeans. They continued doing so afterwards.

Cherokee Indians owning plantations in the American South also owned Negro slaves to work them, which many Cherokee took with them when they moved to what became Oklahoma. In the American Civil War, the Cherokee fought with the South.

Cherokee and Negro interests in that war were clear. White American interests were divided.

Slavery did not inspire the secession of South Carolina and the other Confederate States from the Union. The problem was the primarily Northern abolitionists threatening to abolish slavery without fair compensation, repatriation, and other sensitivity to the massive cultural and economic impacts of abolishing slavery, in a country already deeply divided between North and South. The only thing worse for poor white Americans than bringing in millions of Negro slaves would be releasing them in America.

Other Western countries abolished slavery without war. America's slave states would have done so too, with time and planning.

For his part, President Abraham Lincoln's primary motivation for waging the American Civil War was holding the Union together. Had he responded to the Confederate States' secessions with undertakings not to abolish slavery federally but leave abolition to the states, with which he would negotiate federal government compensation to foster the end of slavery, might Lincoln have persuaded the Confederate States to revoke their secession, even after the first shots were fired at Fort Sumter? Could Lincoln have averted the American Civil War with a law like Britain's Slave Compensation Act of 1837?

As well as money, Lincoln could have offered repatriation of freed slaves to Africa. He could perhaps have offered deportation of Africans to their own black country from the British colonies that later became Belize and Guyana, as Lincoln later contemplated during the Civil War. The Confederate States could secede again later, if Lincoln breached his word.

Britain expended a fortune in wealth ending slavery. America also expended a fortune ending slavery, while suffering more than half a million and possibly a million dead in the American Civil War.

Forming the Confederate States of America was not treason. It was secession. Confederate soldiers, sailors, and civilians were not traitors. They were secessionists.

While the United States of America refused to allow Virginia and other Confederate States to secede from the Union, the state of Virginia allowed West Virginia to secede from the state of Virginia, in 1861. Compatriots do not kill each other to compel them to remain compatriots.

When American Unionists separated nationalism from racism, white people attacked each other. They made race less important than causes, statehood, and nationalities, to all white people's loss and other races' benefit. Nominally holding America together, they ravaged her.

If the greatest motivation driving the Union was not simply the Union but the ideas it embodied, then the American Civil War was America's first war of ideology, if only from the white Unionists' point of view. At the time, those ideas were less about slavery than they have come to seem in retrospect. They were merely ideas nevertheless.

Long before World War II made total war infamous, General William Sherman's March to the Sea during the American Civil War introduced America, if not the world, to total war. We are relaxed about the deadliest war in American history, when we construe it as a war to liberate Africans.

Since then, the West has lost our senses of statehood and nationalities, but we still have ideas to be our causes. We fight each other to aid and defend other races.

The Endless Pursuit of Apology

Amidst our individualism, white people rarely apologise to other white people anymore. Amidst our rejection of racism, we now apologise to everyone else.

We are compelled to identify with our forebears or rest of our race whenever time comes to apologise to another race. We escape white people's past racism with our white people's proud guilt. We are more arrogant than ever to see ourselves rising above race.

While other races do not countenance they could do very much wrong, we do not countenance we could do very much right, except apologise and apologise again. We take responsibility for the failings of our democratically elected governments even if those governments reflect our multiracial citizenry or act outside the mandate of any election. We regret with unwavering humility, even crude arrogance, for being so remorseful.

The past has become passé and we rarely think about it, except being pleased to have left it and deriding white people unpleased, but in our endless pursuit of apology, the only apologies more commonplace than ours for what we think are our present-day failings are ours for what we think were our forebears' failings. Our anti-racial arrogance becomes reason to pillory our past.

We abandon all thoughts of our heritage, except when we sense a chance to regret. Enjoying nothing more than basking in a good apology, we trawl through history books looking for other people's suffering. We then flagellate ourselves.

When we are not neglecting history, we are immersed in it, wallowing in it, but it is a history of remorse. We are races convicted of past wrongfulness, painfully aware we are white. Our histories become longer and longer.

White racial guilt does not contemplate forgiveness, by us of ourselves or by anyone else. It is unending and relentless, not just in our sad sorry eyes but in the angry eyes we inflame in the rest of the world.

People of other races walk by unconcerned. They do not share our passion for guilt. They retain their loyalties: respecting and defending their generations dead before they were born. They defend their race's reputation, as we do not defend ours.

Race and Language

Abbreviations and slang have long been commonplace. Since we began manipulating language for political purposes, we came to presume our forebears did too. Presuming that everything our forebears did was to demean and oppress other races, we presume the same of their slang for other races we now find bitterly offensive.

Our forebears neither demeaned nor oppressed other races. Nor did they exploit language to that end. Those slang terms we now find offensive were innocuous, used by other races too.

No one's sensitivity stops us from using abbreviations for white people, but our linguistic paternalism means we dare not abbreviate the names of other races or anything about them. Even where white people are powerless and subordinate to other races, as we are when we are victims of crimes they commit, we are prohibited from tapering our respect for them with slang abbreviations. We should not be mentioning the race of criminals harming us anyway.

No longer is there even supposed to be a third party collective pronoun "they" regarding another race. There is supposed to be only "we," unless we are berating white people.

Forever yearning for more proof we have rejected our past racism, much of the English language became colourless. Any language that reinforced something positive about being white has been removed, because it supposedly implied something negative about being anything else.

Contrariwise, phrases and sentences have become offensive for removing all hint of race, if they fail to respect people of other races retaining their racial loyalties and sensitivities. Language is for their advancement, not our defence.

Our language is not meant to respect our experiences. It is meant to respect other races' experiences.

With our great sensitivity to race, we encourage other races to be sensitive, picking up our every error when we fall short. We then correct ourselves and apologise.

Language becomes another means of the races we have empowered asserting their power over us, much as we falsely imagine our forebears oppressing them with their language. We can hardly blame other races for exerting the power we grant them, even if our indulgence does not meaningfully profit them.

We worry about white people's words, while other races enjoy their racial epithets to describe white people, especially poor white people. We return to race to berate each other and excuse other races, judging the West as we do not judge other races. Ours are the high standards we must uphold, whatever other races do. We are not empowered to complain about anything.

The Serious Matter of Humour

Of all the oppressions inflicted upon people who might otherwise be free, the cruellest have been those stripping humour from our lives. We treat jokes most seriously because we are very serious people.

The safest course is not to say or do anything referring to someone of another race. It would be petty if we thought racism was petty and be boring if we wanted to laugh, but laughing can be particularly distasteful.

In our frenetic obsession with racism, any hint of race is all that our offence requires. We do not need to know anyone of another race also feeling offence, although it helps.

We are no more forgiving of private conversations than public addresses. Racism is that important.

We are supposed to cease racism with or without an audience. Nobody need suffer, nobody need know, but we still call it wrong. The joke can be inside our heads, but our heads we are trying to change. Hidden in the recesses of unimaginable minds, race should never be alluded to jovially.

The jokes we can make are those about work, wealth, and values: lawyers, aristocrats, and people whose political opinions are not ours. We can joke about racists, but not about race.

Well, other races anyway. We still have white people to mock. The sense of humour we have lost when it comes to any slight upon other races finds full voice and eager audiences when deriding our own. No hair but Western is naturally blonde, or unnaturally blonde to any obvious degree, so we can stereotype blonde women, sometimes blond men, as being stupid.

It is not true, but nobody cares if people start believing that blonde people are stupid, as we might care if people started believing bad things about people of other races, even if those bad things are true. Blonde people do not admit to caring, and might even make the same jokes themselves.

Other races do not joke about themselves. With our support behind them, they joke about us.

Other races are not so fearful of being labelled racist as we are. They do not feel the insult.

Their racism does not excuse our racism; nothing does that. Ours is the racism we are determined to destroy.

Acceptable and Unacceptable Abuse

Since we ceased being racist and became individuals, we lost our connection with each other. We also lost our link with traditional Western etiquette.

We have become more and more abusive. We swear and blaspheme without compunction as our grandparents could not imagine. We tear each other down over anything. Hell, we love abuse, but one whiff less than respectful of other races and we recoil with gut-felt offence.

For the tribeless West, abuse without racism is not really abuse. It is communication.

Abuse with racism is abuse. We call it racial vilification, often making it a criminal offence.

We are not to abuse other races. We are to abuse our race. Abusing white people is acceptable: righteous abuse. It is practically compulsory towards racists.

Abusing other races is not acceptable, even if there are no racial elements intended in the abuse. We make race central to so much of our lives, and become furious when a white person, even a child, forgets.

We indulge other races using derogatory racial epithets unacceptable for us because we indulge other races. When they use those epithets about people of their race, they declare their empowerment to use them we lack.

Nobody cares that people of other races call white people crackas, gringos, honkies, or anything else. We meekly accept derogatory racial epithets against us as more punishment for our supposed racial guilt. We accept people hating us, in more of our punishment for the Holocaust.

When they use racial epithets against people of other races, it is all too problematic for us unable to comprehend anyone but white people being racist. We tend not to think about it. What we do not ignore, we excuse, exonerating other races from racism.

Our vision of a world without race and our embrace of other races often clash with their racism. If we pay attention, then it is to try to save other races from prejudice as we do not try to save our own.

We are normally not so racist as to notice the race of a racist, unless the racist is white. The only racial derision offending us is ours.

Not coincidentally, the white people least abusive towards people generally tend to remain the most racist. They are generally polite, revealing their racism in their opinions without abuse, but with care for their compatriots, countries, and cultures.

They might be least abusive because they feel connected to others of their race. They might thus honour traditional Western culture and thus etiquette.

They might simply be old, when older people are both nicer and more likely to be racist. If we were not so hostile to racism, we might recognise racists to be the most likeable of people.

The most aggressive, abusive, hate-filled people are generally those most opposed to white racism. Abuse vents their hostility to white people, as well as demonstrating their rejection of Western etiquette. They are our most vociferous foes, shouting their hatred to strangers in the street.

Class is never far away. The poorer or most powerless a white person is, in his decrepit council flat or her women's charity shelter, the quicker we are to presume that he or she is racist.

Whatever their politeness, we make racists the rubbish of our race like nobody else. We only call poor racists white trash.

White Supremacy

All over the world, there are races considering their races and cultures superior to others. We have become hostile to any suggestion ours might be.

All races, except us, look down upon races darker than they are. When other races complain about each other, we generally shut those complaints from our mind.

Arabs accuse Jews of racism. We are not about to accuse any race but ours of racism, not since the Holocaust.

The only other hints of racial supremacy about which people complain, or even notice, are those in white people. We have nothing to fear from white supremacists but quake in fear that any remain. In the Jewish mindset and in our mindset scarred by the Holocaust, white supremacy connotes Nazism, although races that fought and defeated Nazism also considered ourselves superior to others.

Loving ourselves for being of our race does not have to be synonymous with a sense of racial supremacy, but white people do not need to consider our race superior to others to be accused of white supremacy. We simply need not to consider ourselves worse.

Uniquely among the races of earth, we feel that not espousing our cultural, aesthetic, or other inferiority equates to some boot-stomping sense of being superior. In practice, white supremacy has become another label to abuse white people not hating our race.

We could instead be kind, allowing ourselves the racial compliments we confer upon others. We need only believe we are as worthy of self-respect as other races are worthy.

Wanting to survive does not require a sense of superiority. It does require some sense of self-worth.

Were people of other races to feel ashamed of their race, we would counsel them, but other races do not need to exhort pride in their race. We refuse to feel pride in ours.

We have everything to fear from Arab, Chinese, and other non-white supremacists, but never so much as contemplate they exist. Nobody accuses them of their particular supremacy, however biologically inferior they consider people darker than they are to be. That would be racist.

Before black nationalists we kneel, or march in their support. Nobody accuses black people of black supremacy, however morally inferior they consider white people to be.

Early in the twenty-first century, we probably are morally inferior. Wantonly we betray our forebears, families, and each other. There is something evil about hating people among our race caring for us.

White Inferiority

White people have become prejudiced against us and our kind, pounding ourselves with self-hating racism. Our uncompromising opposition to white people's racism requires us to denigrate ourselves.

Recoiling repulsed at Nazi talk of racial superiority, we are more comfortable with talk of our supposed racial inferiority. We have come to see other races as better than us.

We abandon our fixation with equality to consider ourselves intrinsically inferior. It is simpler.

By doing so, we recognise racial comparisons, but without any scientific rigour or the discipline of logic. Racial hatred is no less hatred because we hate our own.

Seeing and hearing us often enough, our attitudes to ourselves became other people's attitudes to us. We dumb whiteys are more stupid than ever, destroying our value in ourselves.

We think we are distinct from the rest of our race when it is race by which we malign each other. By race, we malign ourselves. Western self-bigotry we might call our fight against racism, but it is a fight against our race.

Our inversion of racism is still racism. Ours are the politics of self-abuse.

Without faith in our peoples, we cast our adoration elsewhere. All the glory of a race unacceptable if we felt glory for our race becomes acceptable, even admirable, when we latch onto others; our meekness turns back to pride. We adopt other races as our own. Their histories and ancestors, futures and descendants become ours, we imagine.

Identifying with our chosen race, we are no longer post-racial white people. We are racial somebody else. Our post-racial visions are racial, for any race but our own.

Ultimately, our identification with other races has little to do with our attitudes to those races. It has everything to do with our attitudes towards our race.

We escape our racial self-loathing with the arrogance we are greater than people without our frames of mind. With advanced perceptions to which we accredit ourselves, we idolise our individual selves distinct from a sense we are the race we despise: our own. What had been our racial inferiority becomes our new-found sense of personal superiority, but we are no longer ourselves at all.

Whites-Only Racism

Time and again in our tribeless West, when we mix talk of equality with identity, equality gives way to power. We submit to the ever-growing demands of other races, because we think resisting them would be racist.

Whatever the ideologically driven definitions people contrive, ultimately racism is refusing to discriminate against white people or in favour of other races. We have allowed other races to impose upon us definitions of racism by which only white people are racist. However powerful someone of another race might be, with his money or her political office, we insist that person cannot be racist.

However poor and powerless a white person is, in his poverty or her vulnerability, that person can be racist. Only other races can be victims of racism.

We rationalise those definitions by citing supposed structures of privilege based on race, but those structures welcomed other races to the West as no other races have welcomed immigrants to their countries. The best way then for us to help other races is by not admitting them into our countries but by leaving them in their own, where their systems and cultures dominate. Excluding immigrants by their race would not be racist, because they never become subject to our white-dominated cultures.

In practice, we are not so nuanced. We treat Western borders as expressions of white power, to be unwound in pursuit of equality.

Other races can have borders. Equality is for the West.

Without our convictions of equality, other races in countries they inherited do not feel as we feel. They enjoy their privilege, without feeling the passions about racism in their countries we encourage them to feel in ours. Unconcerned about their economic or political dominance, they do not reject their races' racism because theirs is the dominant culture.

We screamed against white South African racism through the time of apartheid. With Africans in control, we are not so fussed about African racism or tribalism: racism coming closer to home.

We believe people of colour are not racist in their countries however they treat us, because we insist ours is the dominant culture on earth. Once, it might have been. Today, it plainly is not.

Even if we realise we are no longer so dominant around the world, we rationalise another reason that only white people are racist: our supposed persecution of other races through history. That one never expires. Events before we were born supposedly mean we cannot relax our rules about race, however completely the West collapses.

If this is our racial punishment, then our futures suffer for what we now deem the failings of our past: our insurmountable burden of history. If Jews are not still punishing us, then we are punishing our pernicious selves.

Too accommodating of Nazi Germany before World War II, defending our races and averting war instead of dying to save Jews, we keep trying to atone. We feel responsible for not saving Jews through the Holocaust, but do not know what more we could have done. Striving to clean ourselves, we stay dirty.

What we think are the crimes of our long racial past require retribution. Other races' loyalty to their ancestors who supposedly suffered so much at our ancestors' hands becomes admirable. If theirs is racism then it is innocent racism.

What then is racism? Racism is white people thinking or feeling about race the way that people of other races remain free to feel and think about it. Racism means, effectively, not hating white people.

The arguments by which only white people are racist are really semantic gymnastics premised upon hostility to white people. Such hostility to white people's racism but justification for all other racism is simply more racial conflict, but one in which white people fight our own.

If only white people are racist, then the whole concept of racism becomes intrinsically racist. It is racist post-racism, in response to which we wage our racist anti-racism. That fundamental inconsistency, that illogic, should be reason enough for the white racist stigma to abate. It has not been so far.

The Presumption of White People's Racism

People's words might reveal their motivations, intentions, and other states of mind, although words can be ambiguous. They can deceive.

Without evidence to warrant the distinction, we presume white people caught up in racial conflict are racists and supremacists. We presume those other races are fighting racism, or simply want space. When other races complain they are suffering discrimination, we presume white people are to blame.

Normally, word of mouth is mere hearsay and a weak form of evidence, but not when accusing white people of racism. So opposed are we to racial discrimination, we surrender our old legal principle: the presumption of innocence. Laws often specify that when a complainant alleges racial discrimination, the onus is on the accused person to prove that he or she was not racist. In allegations of white people's racism, there is a presumption of guilt.

The law is predicated upon only the accused person knowing the thoughts inside his or her head, but the same can be said of people accused of a crime. If that demonstrates the special seriousness with which we treat racism, then we treat it as being more serious than rape and murder. People accused of those crimes retain their presumptions of innocence. The prosecution must provide evidence of their intentions, their *mens rea*, inside their heads.

The burden to prove we are not racist can be hard to overcome, but not always impossible. Without good evidence in our defence, for white people to deny we are racist having been accused of racism is racist.

The best evidence we are not racist is publicly pillorying our race, as if something about that is not racist. We do it over and over.

Conversely, no amount of evidence proves people of another race are racist. With our insistence that only white people are racist, accusing people of other races of being racist is racist.

The big picture for us is our grand perception of white people oppressing other races, as it has increasingly become since the Holocaust. We cannot make any more negative stereotypes of white people than to call each other racist. It is our favourite stereotype, and it presses us to do more to eradicate racism. It presses us even more to pillory our race.

Incredibly diligent in avoiding racist offence, we need to be excruciatingly careful. Others watch us much as we watch them, if they are white. We are quick to pounce when somebody fails.

If it seems like we cannot defend ourselves, then it is because we cannot. Defending ourselves would be racist.

Complaining about it all would be racism. Complaining about anything imposed upon white people to our detriment is racism.

Erasing White People

The rhetorical weapon of choice against white people has become to call white people racist. The R-word swiftly and single-handedly overwhelms all other considerations. Certain that racism poisons everything a racist thinks, nobody should listen to what that person says, or care what that person feels.

People of other races unhappy with anything we do or are not doing need only accuse us of being racist: the button to make white people do or not do whatever other people wish. Fear of the accusation of racism being uttered against us paralyses whole Western populations.

No amount of other races' racism need deter them. Their racism does not deter us.

Racism is a political construction binding white people whichever way we turn. We are far too fearful of being called racists to call people of other races racist, and provoke the racist barb in reply.

The increasing animosity towards white people from immigrants as their numbers grow is thinly or thickly veiled as an effort to eradicate racism. Immigrants we have welcomed to our universities ban white students from their anti-racism events.

Racial bigotry is never more ironic than when cloaked in the guise of opposing racism. When only white people are racist, then campaigns against racism are really campaigns against white people. Fighting racism is fighting white people, by people refusing to admit their prejudice or their part in racial abuse and conflict. Eradicating racism is eradicating white people.

The White Man's Burden

Our Western sense of other races being inferior to us was not hatred or any kind of phobia. It did not lead us to oppress them. Instead, it led us to help them.

In 1899, Englishman Rudyard Kipling's poem 'The White Man's Burden' exhorted, sincerely or satirically, Europeans nobly sacrificing so much to assist other races. Less able to help themselves, Kipling mused, they needed us. We helped them, dying as we did, even if they hated us for it.

Our greatest fault was arrogance. It still is.

With our certain self-assurance, white people still carry the world's problems on our shoulders. Other races are no less aware than we are of wars, poverty, and pestilence elsewhere, but only we think our role is to solve them. Our sense of being white brings us no end of angst.

By thinking we are morally obliged to help other races, we do not sense our goodness. We assume the West is the world, and that the only alternative to our selfishness is saving other races.

Adopting other people's problems as our own, we work to earn money providing for people we never meet. We dispense payments from our bank accounts or credit cards to relieve impoverished other races and aid victims of distant disasters we have seen on the television news.

Our best efforts cannot strip the reality of racial difference from our eyes. We are unashamedly racial with our generosity, providing aid with full regard to the races of the recipients, but they are not our races. Knowing we cannot ignore race, we remain other races' benefactors.

The people we help do not enter into it. We keep being generous because it is our post-racial identity, as much as helping other races was once a feature of our racial identity. We are not sure what we would do without it.

Our post-racial identity is grounded not just in obligation but shame whenever we fall short. We cannot imagine racial loyalty, but have racial shame in abundance.

When we are to blame for our inevitable failings, then we blame each other. We fail to warrant excuse, too arrogant for that.

We cannot do enough. In spite of our great efforts, we feel we should do more. Our white man's burden never ends.

Social Conscience

For people of other races, a social conscience means helping their own. For white people, it means helping them too, within our countries and without: a white man's burden collective upon the West and individual upon each of us. We consider caring about white people to be racist, but offering our helping hands to other races to be humanitarian.

We share our national good with other races, embracing them when we like our countries, but we keep our obligations to ourselves. When our images of other race heroes and heroines give way to thoughts of their poverty, ill health, alcoholism, imprisonment, child abuse, school truancy, or other problems, then only we are responsible for redressing them.

The races we refuse to countenance to benefit us, we recognise to benefit them. While we deride white people proud of their race, we applaud those concerned that other races are still poorer, sicker, or stupider than we are. We have become the people who hate us because the darker a people's race, the greater the mess of their lives.

Rights are for other races. We have obligations. Other races remain absolved of obligation, enjoying only our sympathies.

Poor white people rarely rate a mention. We hold only other races incapable of helping themselves.

Our presumption that other races cannot rescue themselves tells them they cannot. People are rational, up to a point. If people do not need to strive then they will not. If we tell people they are not accountable for their actions, they are not.

We expend a disproportionate amount of time, money, and effort upon other races' health, education, and other well-being, because neither they nor we hold them accountable for their shortcomings. Accountability is ours alone.

When colonial Europeans give indigenous people money without them needing to work, they do not work. The resulting social problems, much greater than any from European colonisation, only add to our sense we should do more to help them.

Other beneficiaries of our burden might already be rich, but all the more credit to them for working hard and being clever, overcoming their affliction. They have not chosen their race any more than we chose ours. It is the most perverse white supremacy, while we loathe our past racism.

Foreign Aid

No other race has helped more people than white people have helped through history and are still helping. We are the most generous race on earth, without being so racist as to notice.

Only the West insists rich countries are obliged to help poor countries, presuming that only we are so rich, along sometimes with Japan. The trillions of dollars that the West has dished out in foreign aid since World War II has not achieved very much. With our white man's burden in mind, we insist the failure of foreign aid is our fault. We keep handing out more, while cutting pensions and other money for white people.

The costs of white racial generosity and grand social consciences are not borne by our rich but our lowly, who forgo opportunities for better healthcare, education, and housing so we can give them to other races. The services we provide other races are fewer services we provide our poor. The time and money we expend improving other races' lives we do not spend improving the lives of our own.

Dealing with other races' problems distracts us from dealing with white people's problems. We remain indifferent to our compatriots' loneliness, vulnerability, and despair, although we comfort other races every time.

Conversely, the beneficiaries of our foreign aid are not primarily the poor of other races but their elite. No wonder rich people from rich and poor countries alike want us to give more.

We do not identify with the rest of our race, so do not feel like we are giving our wealth away. Our rich and middle classes might suffer a little more taxes because we give away foreign aid, but we are redistributing wealth we do not notice; we might not be rich but do not feel like we are poor. The white people's wealth we are most keen to redistribute is the wealth of other white people.

Countries outside the West do not imagine being subject to any sense of obligation as we do. They do not share our drive for equality. While the West gives our money away, oil-rich Arab emirates indulge themselves.

Those countries that aid foreigners do so to further their national objectives and interests. Oil-rich Arabs can be generous donors, but only to fellow Arabs and Muslims.

Other races discriminate. We do not. East Europeans would have welcomed racial loyalty from the West, but we are much less interested in the needs of white people than the desires of other races.

Arabs are planning for their future after oil. We are not planning for a future at all.

International Socialism

In response to National Socialism, Nazism, and the Holocaust, the West embraced international socialism. We rejected the nationalism while adopting the socialism.

Ours is not the socialism of common purpose and ownership within a race, as it was in Nazi Germany and remains among other rich races and in the cries of national communism in Asia. Ours is an interracial socialism: the socialism of sameness.

Our forefathers and mothers created wealth and lifestyles they bequeathed to us, but so sure have we become that races are equal, we think the West cannot have prospered so well in the past because of our ingenuity, enterprise, or hard work. We cannot have succeeded by our science, engineering, or innovation, we think. No mental or physical superiority could have let us conquer the earth with grand empires.

Instead, with the West unwilling to believe that some races might be smarter or more industrious than others, the only explanation remaining for the wealth our forebears created is their supposed oppression of others. Oppression by race, we call racism.

Why some other races were richer than others, we do not consider. We discard our forebears' good characters in a grand generalisation they were bad, as we would never accept about other races.

The same can be said for racial differences in the present. We believe that other races are poorer than we are because we exploit them, without thought of races richer than we are or thought of the relative riches of other races.

We feel guilt for achievement. We damn ourselves for success.

What we feel about races we should feel about individuals, if we insist everyone is the same. If the West cannot have succeeded so well by our innate abilities or diligence but by exploiting other races, then neither can one person succeed except by exploiting another.

Karl Marx understood as much when he developed communism (totalitarian socialism) in the nineteenth century, interpreting differences by class much as we now think about differences by race. Embracing international socialism makes little sense without embracing communism locally. Racial equality requires it.

Equality

We became obsessed with equality and pursuit of still more, except that the equality we want is not between rich and poor white people. Nor is it between rich and poor people generally.

Equality consumes the West, but it is racial equality. The racial equality we pursue is between races, not within them.

Seized by the reality of race, racial equality presupposes race. Race remains.

We do not just think races are equal in every conceivable way. We want them to be.

Other races are not interested in equality, unless it betters them. They do not want the equality that would bring their people down.

We do. Equality means everything to us, but only at white people's expense.

We equate equity to equality, certain that any apparent inequality cannot be due to real inequality but to something unfair. Increasingly driving our foreign, economic, and social policy since the Second World War is our sense it is only fair that we thieves give away our ill-gotten inheritances and earnings, be it through welfare, immigration, or commerce.

Other races we see not as beneficiaries of our benevolence but as victims of our supposed oppression. We are freely giving our wealth to other races, but feel only guilt for what we have not yet given.

When we blame our racism for other races' failings and misadventures, we increase our burden to compensate them. Payments to other races are not presents but reparations.

When other races blame our racism for their failings, they lighten their burden to redress them. They reduce their responsibilities still further.

White people think we can make everyone equal, but we have spent centuries helping other races without making much improvement with some. White people willing to work and subsidise other races by taxation and donation cannot make equal what is unequal.

Races are not naturally equal. They are naturally different. Racial equality is an insatiable desire we can never discharge.

We confuse justice with equality. Espousing equality creates feelings of injustice among people less intelligent, talented, or hard-working than others. They will only achieve equality if it is forced upon people smarter, more skilled, and more industrious than they are. That was communism.

Thus equality is extremely unfair. It imposes the injustice of taking from smarter, more skilled, and more industrious people to give to the rest.

It does so between people. It does so between races.

When people without nationalism, racism, or other tribal connections share everything they have, they all end up with nothing. When the clever and energetic live as well as the stupid and lazy, people are stupid and lazy. Talented, intelligent, and industrious people soon stop trying, thinking, and working.

Equality means they can all suffer equally. With their silver lapel pins and brooches, rich white individuals might cease being so benevolent when the last wealth to give up is theirs.

Anti-White Discrimination

While white people increasingly insisted races were not real after the Holocaust, people of other races never ceased knowing that races are real. While white people refused to defend our racial interests for being racism, other races grew in number. Increasingly, those other races asserted their racial interests: their racism.

Those other races learnt the language of the West. When they complained that white people discriminated against them, we believed them. When they demanded more in the name of equality, we succumbed. We thus allow discrimination in their favour, at the expense of our own.

Discrimination remains. We do not grant everyone equality of opportunity, confident that the equality of races will lead to an equality of outcomes, because it has not led to equality so far. Unable to imagine races being different, we conclude some races fare worse than we fare because white people remain unfairly politically and economically powerful. We think being white makes competing merely on merit intrinsically unfair.

For all our Western democracies decrying discrimination *against* other races, we are willing to discriminate *for* them. The only discrimination we countenance is that favouring other races. It must, of necessity, disadvantage ours. Our post-racial discrimination discriminates against our own.

So-called affirmative action includes minimum quotas reserved to non-white races in educational institutional admissions, employment, business contracts, and so forth. They might speak of positions and contracts being reserved to minorities, but they do not benefit white people where we are minorities. They are quotas for other races' minimum success, and thus limits to our maximum success.

We never lose our racial natures, but ours is the racism of rejecting our own. White people compete without compromise with each other, while offering charity to everyone else.

We do not want advantage, so accept disadvantage. Our rejection of racism requires us not to ignore race, but to promote people from other races because of their race: immigrant privilege.

Other races are not as eager as we are to take backward steps, not even when merit is the reason. Nor are they a single generic group. Lacking our senses of obligation and equality, other races are not as eager as we are to disadvantage their own to help other races.

An immigrant race might support affirmative action in one context operating to its advantage, but oppose affirmative action in another context operating to its advantage. That is not hypocrisy. It is simply racial self-interest, as white people cannot comprehend.

The racial equality we pursue is one by which white people are not faring better than other races. We can fare worse.

Merit only comes into it within races. The discrimination we want is not so much against us individually. It is against other white people.

We recognise other races to help them, and our own race to excuse us from responsibility to help. We are not so racist as to care about white contractors and candidates whose attributes or experience would have entitled them to success, but who fail because of our discrimination.

We disempower weaker white people because powerful white people enjoy so much, punishing weaker white people into powerlessness, while we empower other races. The years since 1945, if not beforehand, have been a continual story of white people empowering other races and disempowering each other, unaware that we are disempowering ourselves. Ours is a powerlessness perversely foisted upon us by race.

The New White Identity

White people spent decades after the Holocaust pretending that race does not exist. Other races indulged our pretence when it was reason for the West to admit more of them as immigrants, but the time came there were enough of them to dismiss the pretence. We keep admitting more of them anyway.

Early in the twenty-first century, pretending that races do not exist became more of our supposed white privilege: expecting other races to ignore race because we do. They insist we remember.

We have been letting other races tell us what being white should mean since the Holocaust. Our new white identity is devoted to dismantling the so-called privilege of being white. We have no other purpose.

White privilege is white people with anything left not yet given to other races. White privilege is simply being white.

It is a perception that blames all the inequalities in the world on white people's supposed oppression of others, now and in the past, while taking on the burden of redressing them: helping other races until they possess all that we possess, and more. It is our white man's burden without the qualification our self-respect used to be. It is our drive for equality with a past in which our wealth was ours.

Our sense of ourselves became our deference to others. For all our dreams of racial harmony and equality raising other races high, we know our dreams are failing. Subjugating ourselves to the aid of other races is our rehabilitation, but never seems to help. We are too far shamed from liking anything about us.

Such a feeling of obligation to help other races is a luxury for white people wealthy enough to afford it. Poor white people have less, if anything, for which to feel ashamed.

It is also something for the young, who believe what they have been told about race. Older people remember history that younger people are not being taught. They and their forebears worked for their wealth. They helped people, without oppressing anyone.

Poor White People

Collective identities remain. Measuring wealth by racial totalities, the richest or poorest individuals do not come into it.

White people can be destitute and alone, but still be accorded the burden of being so rich a race. Poor, uneducated, and other vulnerable white people are the fodder for our drive to racial equality.

Our poor are not studying or working as we invite other races to study and work. They might have their payments of welfare, but few people encouraging them to free themselves from dependence. They are not building lives or creating arts but are awfully alone, stumbling about.

The only people who might help poor and powerless white people are rich and powerful white people, but we are busy helping everyone else. We could do so much with our wealth to help them, but we neglect them.

Our ideologies of inclusion are for other races, not ours. Malcontent white people do not understand.

The poor of other races enjoy the rich of their race and us, especially the wealthy white people they never meet, to help them. Poor white people have almost no one. Poverty strains white people as it does not strain the poor of other races because we are alone, driven apart from each other. Our poor are not the beneficiaries of anyone's prejudice.

Wealthy people do not generally regard poor white people as their enemy. They generally do not think about them at all.

When rich people do think about poor white people, they are the trailer park trash, with only themselves to blame for their problems. Rich people presume poor white people's poverty and suffering are within their control; they too could succeed and be rich but they squander their chance, their privilege being white. Aristocrats and public company boardrooms demonstrate the world is for white people, meaning that poor white people have no excuses.

Poor white people in collapsible homes do not feel their racism is to blame for people of other races not joining country clubs or failing to become partners in major accountancy firms. They do not feel the inequalities of the world are their fault, as powerful white people do.

Ours is a racial response to racial inequalities, advancing racial equality by bringing white people down along with other races up. The rich of other races becoming richer at the expense of poor white people means their races become richer and ours become poorer, but no number of poor white people or rich of other races keeps us from feeling white wealth is unjust.

We sacrifice white people poorer than we are to prove it. We sacrifice each other, until we sacrifice ourselves.

White Racial Decline

Amidst our arrogance, powerful white people think they do not need anyone's help. They are wrong.

The only difference between rich and poor people is money, which can seem little difference to save us from the streets. But for the money they represent, jobs and clothes mean even less.

Between our rich and our poor, white middle classes share the arrogance and despair. The class once central to Western prosperity is fading.

We live solitarily, even pointlessly, but aside from our poor we live comfortably, whatever the consequences. Even if we realise that white people are no longer the most affluent people on earth, we find races worse off than we are and help them.

We care more for other races than we care for each other. Helping white people would be racist.

If our race was the most impoverished race on earth, we would look into our past, see how well our forebears did, and do more to help other races. We would find the worse off among other races and help them rather than be so racist as to help sick, weak, or poor white people. Nor would we be so racist as to notice more powerful and affluent races unwilling to help as we do.

We do not lament our racial decline. Keen to gloat with our downfall, we welcome racial equality. We are recompensing other races for our past ruling so much of the world. A future dominated by other races creates equality across human history.

Put simply, there is no friend we will not abandon, crime we will not tolerate, home we will not surrender, or lifestyle we will not sacrifice to prove our unyielding abhorrence of racism. We are so damned proud of our Western fall.

The peoples we are helping are poor to be sure, but they are young peoples. When the West has become too aged to keep helping them, who else will help other races?

Did our help mean much anyway, except to us? They might not care we have gone.

Making Peace with our Past

There is something uncommonly cruel about the way we malign our forebears, who wanted the best for us. They were good men and women with far more honour than we will ever practice or see practiced around us, but we damn them for the racism we respect in other races. We do not pursue knowledge about them and their circumstances that do not fit our vision of history.

Instead, we tear down statues of our most famous forebears or let continue the environment in which others pull their statues down. There was good reason for those statues to have been erected, respecting not just their subjects but all of us they represented.

Our prejudices against our forebears deny us scope to assess their thoughts and deeds fairly. It is a massive injustice against them and against us, manipulating us in our dealings with other races and in our sense of ourselves.

More than our shame is our pride as we assail our shameless forebears, their bronze likenesses crashing to the ground or into the water, knowing they were racists. We think we are better than they were, we solitary pinnacles of how wonderful we are, without being so racist as to think we are better than other races.

Happy people make peace with their past, reconciling themselves with themselves. We are at war with ours, consumed with falsehoods about our preceding generations.

The great travesties of the world are not what we think our forebears did to other races or what we think we are doing to other races now, but what we are now doing to ourselves. Instead of ruefully regretting our ancestors' actions, we will come to rue ours. Saying we are worthy of self-love, our forebears loved us more than we love ourselves, offering us self-affection we are stridently determined to deny.

Our rejection of our forebears is our despair at being alive. We have lost the joy of having come into existence.

Instead, we could leave other races to form and express their views about us and our forebears, without us telling them to hate ours and without them deciding we should hate ours too. We need only defend and seek knowledge of the facts.

If we have racial guilt, then so does every other race for its wars, genocides, and other wrongs. If they have racial pride, then we should have racial pride for the good things we have done. Without denying our blunders, we can feel the merits in what our kin achieved: our heroes and heroines.

If we are not yet willing to feel pride in our people and past, we can at least accord them fair value. We can see the good as well as the bad in our forebears. We can see the bad as well as the good in other people's forebears, presuming neither goodness nor badness of anyone.

Somewhere beyond shame and pride, we could simply appreciate being us, worthy of our affection. Denying our children the chance to love themselves is the cruellest and most horrific abuse.

A Gentle Touch of Racism

Learning to live around the Holocaust does not mean forgetting the Holocaust. It means remembering everything else.

Love and loyalty for a person's race need not be derision or animosity towards other races. We can simply be caring for our race, especially our poor, elderly, and other vulnerable.

White people valuing their race are not impugning anyone. Racism need only be reason, fact, and fairness applied to matters of race.

Racism is recognising race. Racism is also loyalty to our own. There is no shying away from the fact that wanting our race to survive is racist.

The problem that the tribeless West has with racism is that we do not have enough of it. What we have, we direct not for us, but against us.

Had the Holocaust not broken us, the West would still consider familial, racial, and religious loyalty virtues, as other races continue to do. We too would remain wary of outsiders. Such wariness is rational.

Rather than individual self-interest or narrow-minded regionalism, we would speak up for broad-minded nationalism expressed with a desire to keep out of war, as we did through the 1930s. We would honour our dead we have come to dismiss.

Descendants eventually become ancestors. When we honour our ancestors, we invite our descendants to honour us.

We cannot resume loving other races until we resume loving our own. We should feel good when we are good.

Racial loyalties do not mean we wantonly abandon our friends from other races. It means we stand with strangers from our race.

Unlike much of the rest of the world but being the good people we are, our racial loyalties need not neglect other races' interests. Our race's interests need simply prevail, at least a little, above theirs. We can care about our fortune and misfortune.

We can wish other races every happiness and success, but not at our expense. In a world of finite resources, the smartest, most skilled, and hardest working people deserve more than others. They should have the right to earn and keep wealth for their families and race.

When we care about people, we could care about white people too, without meaning others harm. Weary of the white man's burden, Western social consciences could mean caring about white people suffering socially, politically, or economically: aiding our own without malice to others. When our people hurt, we can help them, instead of damning them for their paltry weak failings. We can consider their material comforts and human satisfaction, peace of mind and security walking the streets. All they might fear is being alone.

One day, striving to improve other white people's lots in life, they might help us in return, if required. That is racism.

2. OF WHOM WE'RE BORN:
RACE AND FAMILY

Human beings are born to be racist. By the age of fifteen months, babies show racial bias in choosing playmates. They prefer their own.

Instead of respecting our racial natures, the West has set about erasing our natural racism, but only in white people. Revelations of racist babies and children led educators to devise strategies to weed white girls of four and five years of age from playing with white dolls.

Girls of colour could play with dolls of their colours. There seems hardly any reason to make white dolls anymore.

From 2002 onwards, the British government required schoolteachers to monitor children for racism and schools to report all racist incidents to their local authorities. The reports named the alleged perpetrators and victims, described the incidents, and set out the punishments.

Ours is the wonderful West, where children are no longer punished for much for fear of harming their fragile self-esteem and because we do not judge people. Educational authorities treat children hitting each other as merely situations, which adults are supposed to discuss with the children without punishing them.

Yet children are punished for exhibiting racism, whatever the impact upon their self-esteem. Racists we judge, even when they are children, but not people hitting each other.

Not even murder is punished as racism is. Children can kill other children without suffering criminal records into their adulthood, but records of their racism or other discrimination are passed from one school to another whenever children change schools and are maintained into their adulthood. They can be used if potential employers or universities ask schools for references about them.

More than thirty-four thousand schoolchildren were reported for racist and other discriminatory incidents in England and Wales in the 2009 to '10 year. That included more than twenty thousand children in primary schools. Some children reported in nursery schools were no more than three years of age.

For their part, local authorities monitored the numbers of racist and other discriminatory incidents. They searched for any patterns and took measures to redress them.

Knowing that children are racist, local authorities refused to accept school principals saying there had been no incidents of racism at their schools. Authorities criticised those principals for under-reporting racism.

There is no limit to our determination to eradicate race. In 2008, the National Children's Bureau acknowledged that young people had the ability to recognise different people in their lives. It set about destroying that ability. It wanted adults to discipline young children forming relationships with children from their own race. Adults should also combat racism in toddlers and babies.

Other Western countries are more subtle than Britain. They are no less determined.

The time might come that an ultrasound examination of a pregnant woman's womb will seek signs of racism. The foetus might flinch in response to a foreign food the mother ate. There may be a flicker when the immigrant doctor is a little too rough examining her. It might be enough that the baby is white.

Biological Individualism

Believing that race is no more than a social or political construct, we think that if we do not mention race, no one will notice. If people no longer notice, we think race no longer exists.

Race exists. Children notice.

Races are biological relationships between people: biological connectedness. Racism is one expression of our innate tribalism.

The problem, the West decided after the Holocaust, is that anything biologically linking us together divides us from others. Our rejection of race is a rejection of biological tribalism.

Our indoctrination against racism all seems to work. Children change, or at least claim to have changed.

By one means or another, white people around the West have been stripped of the natural racism enjoyed by other races. Yet race remains intrinsic to the way human beings see each other. Contact between races remains mentally challenging and cognitively draining. Racial diversity imposes a constant tension around us.

Prejudice need not be overt or intentional, but prejudice against outsiders remains innate to humans, even among people caring deeply about equality, as we in the West do. Our natural prejudices remain for people like us, keeping outsiders at a distance.

Yet, we are unwilling to succumb to prejudice. Rather than forming relationships within our race, we form no relationships at all. That is individualism.

Reasons for War

We blame World War II on racism with the Holocaust in mind, although almost universal recognition of racial differences did not drive countries other than Germany or Japan to war. We have long lost interest in Japanese racism.

Much of Europe's feeling of superiority ended with the Great War, until Nazism revived it for Germany. Nazi Germany shared her sense of racial superiority with the British, Dutch, and Scandinavians, which does not make us investigate Nazi thinking. It serves only to lump us accidental accomplices together.

Japan did not share its sense of racial superiority with other races. It still does not.

In Europe, World War II owed more to desires for equality than feelings of superiority. Feeling injustice at the Treaty of Versailles stripping her of land and soul in 1919, Germany's yearning to be treated as the equals of France and Britain facilitated the rise of Nazism in the first place.

We equate racism with the Holocaust, but the problem with racial conflict is not the racism but the conflict. The problem with genocide is the homicide, not the racism.

Instead of being a call to war, the end of racism was supposed to end war. It did not. War does not need race.

People who condone violence bash and murder for any number of reasons. Opposing racism means we replace one motivation with another: wars against racism instead of wars defending our race. Ending white racism just added more reasons to fight.

Hatred, greed, and cruelty remain. There is still killing and pillage, but not racist killing and pillage.

People kill if they find killing acceptable: to keep whatever they value or to get more. People make war for all manner of motivations.

Communist War

In this Age of Ideology, we of the West value ideology. We tarnish feelings of racial superiority with the brush of war, but communist senses of ideological superiority killed more people than feelings of racial superiority ever did. Espousing ideologies of pacifism does not make someone peaceful.

For all the communist focus upon economic commonality around class, ideology matters more. The dictatorship of the proletariat is only of the communist proletariat: of the communists.

Causes of killing were ideological across the crumbling Russian Empire through the end of World War I and across Europe thereafter. The Soviet Union's rejection of racism did not deter it from invading eastern Poland in 1939.

After World War II, German communists murdered fellow Germans trying to escape East Germany. Communist North Korea invaded South Korea in 1950. North and South Vietnamese communists waged the Vietnam War from 1955. In defence of communism from reform or challenge, the Soviet Union invaded Hungary in 1956, Czechoslovakia in 1968, and Afghanistan in 1979.

Instead of racial superiority, doctrines of racial and other equality have underpinned the numerous communist atrocities. If we reject racism for the millions of deaths at the hands of Nazism, we should reject equality for the tens of millions dead at the hands of communism. The Holocaust was no more the logical consequence of racism than the many communist massacres were the logical consequence of sharing lunch with a friend. They both required a willingness to kill, with little or no compunction.

We used to think democracies were less likely to make war than dictatorships, but our histories, especially our recent histories, suggest otherwise. Western opponents of communism proved as ideological as the communists: engaging in other people's wars, willing to give up our races and countries, all for ideological reasons. Since World War II, Western governments have sent their young men to fight and die not for their countries and races but to defend other countries and races.

Science

Before being corrupted by ideology and political objectives, science was a methodical pursuit of the truth. Science was objective.

Our aim was knowledge; we tried to understand. Knowledge was subjective, vulnerable to error but growing as we learnt.

We questioned and investigated. If the facts did not accord with what we thought was the truth, then we needed to think more. We had probably been wrong.

Science allowed us to develop theories and improve our knowledge in the light of new information. When the evidence allowed it, and for as long as it did, we were certain.

Among the impressions we took from the Holocaust was the supposed danger of certainty, however that certainty came about. Uncertainty, we felt, demanded tolerance.

A few months after the end of the Holocaust, the two atom bombs America dropped on Japan ended the war sooner than it would otherwise have ended. Instead of appreciating the many lives they saved, the bombs left the West more fearful than ever.

It was the end of certainty. The age of science was over, as regards anything important.

The West stopped believing in facts. Without facts, there can be no conviction. Without conviction, we cannot care enough to conflict.

We confuse objective facts with subjective knowledge. Relativism is our rejection of reality: our rejection of science.

The Politicisation of Science

Relativism does not just mean there are no realities. It also means professing realities that are not reality at all, when talk about each person's reality falls away.

Increasingly since the Second World War, our purpose in science has ceased being to determine the facts. It has become to affirm what we believe facts should be.

Facts and knowledge become synonymous. Instead of knowledge of the world, we seek verification of our beliefs.

We have replaced the precision of scientific analysis with political objectives. To that end, people have politicised science. Postmodern science is science as a tool of political objectives, because everything is a tool of political objectives, in this Age of Ideology.

The ideological West has proceeded from certainty through uncertainty back to certainty again. Our ideological orthodoxies cannot comprehend questioning and investigating, at least about anything important.

Whereas our old certainty was based upon evidence, our new certainty is based upon ideology. Whereas our old certainty was based upon intellect, our new certainty is based upon emotion: our need to believe. Ideologies hold firm whatever the evidence otherwise.

When facts do not accord with our ideology, we discard the facts, fobbing away perceptions that do not suit our ideological convictions. We base our beliefs not upon the evidence, but in spite of it.

We meekly conceal undesirable facts or reduce them to mere theories. Conversely, we promote desirable theories as if those theories were facts: determined by consensus and majority opinions among people who already agree.

In such an environment, people are experts because they say they are experts. They denote the most nonsensical of statements scientific, because they want them to be.

They invent whole fields of supposed science for no other purpose than to deem their nonsensical beliefs scientific. Conversely, they dismiss whole fields of real science, most notably about human biology, as antiquated stereotypes, religious dogma, or political constructs.

In our lives without science, facts are not just immaterial. They can be offensive.

The ideological West rejects reality, whenever reality could cause offence. We make reality whatever we want reality to be.

Ours is the age of unreality. Reality is virtual.

The politicisation of science corrupts our knowledge, but facts do not change for what anyone says. We are condemned to error and ignorance.

Eugenics

Not only do we use notions of science to advance our political objectives, we assume our forebears did too. We think white people constructed biological distinctions between people to divide and oppress, because (since the Holocaust) we think our forebears did everything to oppress. It is a falsification of history into a story of white people's wickedness, but there is something particularly nonsensical about saying any race or group of races invented the concept of race, as if there would have been no races otherwise: racism without race.

All the peoples of the world recognised race as soon as they encountered people of another race, just as they recognised all the observable differences between people the West now downplays. Tribes barely able to do more than drag sticks in the sand distinguished different races they saw, even if only in the most obviously observable differences, whatever words they happened to use to describe them.

Race had been referred to for centuries as we might speak of nations, before the West's increasingly sophisticated sciences in the seventeenth century focused upon physical and psychological differences and similarities between peoples. We applied a sense of science to people, much as we applied science to everything else.

Through the ensuing centuries, the West led the way in understanding race because we led the way in rational thought. It was the Age of Enlightenment.

No less than our forebears, the great advocate for the oppressed and founder of communism Karl Marx recognised that races differ in their abilities and capacities to contribute to civilisation. Arguably, race underlay the economic classes and production through which Marx interpreted history.

Marx might have imagined overcoming the biological differences between races, but biological differences they were. Among the many races that Marx and his Prussian collaborator Friedrich Engels disparaged were Jews, of whom Marx was one.

Imagining more than one race developing on earth might seem biologically extraordinary, but just one race developing on earth is no less extraordinary. The circumstances that brought about one lifeform could just as extraordinarily have brought about many lifeforms.

Charles Darwin inspired his polymathic cousin Sir Francis Galton in 1883 to categorise the science of people by their inherited characteristics as eugenics. The Greek word "*genos*" encompasses family and race: those to whom we were born. A combination of inherited features and environmental factors shape people and the choices they make.

Across the scientific world, eugenics was about marriage, babies, and bettering human beings. The honorary vice president of the First International Congress of Eugenics in 1912 was Britain's future bulwark against Nazism, Winston Churchill. Other prominent supporters of the congress included Alexander Graham Bell, the inventor of the telephone. Race was an aspect of eugenics.

The End of Inquiry

Our age of inquiry ended with the Jewish Holocaust. Treating Jewish and other prisoners like laboratory rats, physician Josef Mengele performed crude medical experiments at the Auschwitz-Birkenau concentration camp. We have come to presume that Nazi experimentation was all about racial superiority. It was not. Most haunting were Mengele's experiments involving twins and disease.

A Polish Jew working with Mengele devised a word that would, for the West, become synonymous with race: genocide. Repulsed by the Holocaust, we are repulsed by race. Without race, there is no racism, but if there were really no races, there could be no genocide.

By his callous actions pursuing knowledge indifferent to the suffering involved, Mengele did not just torture and kill. The pursuit of knowledge that hitherto brought the West greatness fell into disrepute, at least about human biology.

We decided knowledge was inseparable from the use of that knowledge: its consequences. Instead of garnering knowledge of heredity with conscience, we gave up on knowledge. We cannot exploit knowledge for evil if we do not have knowledge to start with, so we shut down our sense of inquiry. Knowledge, be damned.

Our postmodern approaches to people are not the product of science or reason. They are political constructions. Never is our politicisation of knowledge more blatant than in relation to human biology.

Postmodern relativism does not apply to matters of race. There is no room for different perspectives, no multitude of truths. We think not with faith but conviction, more resolute than belief merely in God. While we might argue to and fro about deity, there is no argument about race.

We insist race is not real. From our perspective, but not from theirs, Europeans and Jews become two shades of the multitudes. Since the Holocaust, we think that is worthwhile.

Those who think that powerful white people of the past invented race to oppress other races have it back to front. Increasingly since the Second World War, powerful people have insisted race is not real to coax white people out of our racism.

Race is not a political or social construct. The end of race is. Human authorities erase race not because race is not real, but in order to erase racism, at least among white people.

Our ideologies of inclusion, individualism, and equality cannot change the science of people, the biology, but they help us ignore it. We are desperately trying to stop white people being racist.

We rejected racism not on scientific grounds but emotional ones, forged in the flames of the Holocaust, but the pursuit of knowledge was not all bad. In 1940, Nazi German scientists were the first to link smoking tobacco with cancer. Several decades would pass before the Western public learnt the same thing, while tobacco company executives kept their knowledge to themselves.

Genes

Human biology became offensive. Words like Negro and Mongoloid became offensive for reflecting a clinical, scientific approach to race, although we make exemptions in cases like the United Negro College Fund, founded in 1944, for historical reasons. After all, the Fund helps Negroes, who do not mind the name.

Only among white people is race an old concept and even then, only sometimes. Other races retain race and eugenics, even if they do not call it eugenics. China operates formal eugenics programmes.

In our desire to be everything that science at Auschwitz-Birkenau was not, the West ended talk of eugenics for people, although eugenics centred upon creating people rather than killing them. In some cases, eugenics meant sterilising people we thought carried genetic deformities. Without eugenics, we are still sterilising people, but for other reasons.

From eugenics came genes, the more we understood the biological nature of people and our inherited characteristics. We retain a touch of eugenics when we screen sperm donors for genetic diseases.

Genes account for seventy percent of gender-atypical behaviour in people of both genders. Genes might affect specific behaviours in people, such as their associations with people of the other gender or their rejection of limits upon their behaviour.

Inherited traits account for one-fifth of the differences in children's academic performance, after adjusting for environmental factors. Genetic links in women affect their likelihood of forming addictions.

Genes affect people's kindness and caring. They might also affect the risk of autism.

Where there are genes, there used to be race. What is true of individuals is true of races.

Africans are more likely than Europeans to carry the blood type causing sickle cell disease. Conversely, that blood type protects people against malaria.

Among Ashkenazi Jews, genetic mutations significantly increase the risks of women developing breast cancer and ovarian cancer. Researchers have recommended general genetic testing for the presence of the mutations among the entire Ashkenazi population in Israel. Our fear of genetic research into people is our fear of another Holocaust.

Genes and Race

Depending on our definitions, genetic differences between races are at least one percent of the thirty thousand or so genes in human beings. By such a measure, genetic differences between human beings and chimpanzees are less than two percent.

Race is not simply a matter of physical appearance or people's perceptions. It is a matter of blood, biology, and biological relationship.

Variations in three hundred and seventy-seven genotypes suggest that differences between individuals within a population account for ninety-three to ninety-five percent of genetic variation and that differences between major groups (what we might call races) constitute from three to five percent. Genetic differences between ethnic groups within larger racial groups, such as Swedes in Europe and the Hmong in Asia, are about fifteen percent.

There are those in the West who reject race because the range of behaviours, features, and traits within races often exceeds the differences between races. Theirs is a rejection of statistical variances.

In effect, they assert, for example, that one race being on average taller than another race is immaterial because some individuals are taller than other individuals by a greater extent. It is more than saying Zulus are the same as Pygmies because we find a tall Pygmy taller than a short Zulu. It is enough if the difference between the average heights of Zulus and Pygmies is less than the range of heights among Zulus or among Pygmies, even if the shortest of Zulus is still taller than the tallest of Pygmies.

We reject biological race because we reject biological generalisation, although we do not apply such a strict rationale to matters other than race. We do not reject a link between smoking tobacco and lung cancer because a smoker does not contract cancer and a non-smoker does. We do not suggest climatic seasons are not real because some days in winter are warmer than some days in summer, or because the range of temperatures within summer and winter is greater than the difference between average summer and average winter temperatures.

Our rejection of race is Western individualism. Anything less than a one hundred percent genetic difference between races means we reject race as a biological concept, but we are also rejecting race where there is a hundred percent difference between races. It is abundantly clear some physical traits occur throughout some races but not others. Psychological traits might too.

Selective Genetics

When we in the West investigate genes in people early in the twenty-first century, we set careful limits to avoid promoting racism. We have no limits looking for reasons to reject racism.

There are three billion base pairs in each genome (encoded in deoxyribonucleic acid, D.N.A.) known to vary from person to person. People with common sequences in their genome have common ancestors, with the longer the common sequence the more recent their common ancestor.

The shortest common sequences suggest a common ancestor between people as much as a hundred generations or three thousand years ago. People in Britain generally share one such sequence with each other but are slightly less than twenty percent likely to share such a sequence with someone in Turkey. What ought to be evidence for the biological reality of race became more reason instead for us to insist everyone is related.

We feel no affinity with our great-grandparents born less than a century before us, or even our grandparents or parents still with us, but we grab any chance to feel related to other races because of a chance less than one in five we share ancestors who died three thousand years ago. We do not identify with our first and second cousins born of our race, but identify with people who might possibly be our one-hundredth cousins because they are not of our race.

The more that race is biologically real, the more we insist it is not. While we hone in upon particular genes to imagine everyone being related to each other, other races hone in upon genes proving we are not.

Christian Maronites claim ancestry from the seafaring Phoenicians. More than three thousand years after they settled in Lebanon is not enough time for them to share a common identity with Arabs.

We interpret genes to dismiss tribes and races. Other races interpret genes to define them.

While we imagine wealth reducing racism and other biological tribalism, American Indian wealth since they began operating casinos on their reservations in the 1980s accentuated their biological tribalism. Not so keen to share their riches with others as we are, Indian tribes cast off people not of their tribe. Tribes cancel their tribal citizenship, financial entitlements, right to vote in tribal elections, and children's access to tribal schools.

In 1866, Cherokee Indians signed a treaty with the American government awarding their freed Negro slaves tribal citizenship, irrespective of whether the Negroes carried Cherokee blood. In 2011, the Cherokee Supreme Court supported the tribe's right to redefine Cherokee citizenship to exclude the descendants of those Negroes, known as Freedmen, who could not prove they had Cherokee blood relations. This was a biological definition completely unconcerned with anything cultural. The tribe expelled two thousand eight hundred Negro Freedmen.

Indian tribes also expel mixed-tribe Indians whose forebears identified with other tribes. Tribal governments pay companies to examine people's genes.

Tolerance is Western, the American Indians point out. Indian tribes do not tolerate. They turn their backs on people.

So do Australian Aborigines. Aboriginal mothers fearing violence from other Aborigines abandoned mixed-race babies. They also abandoned babies born of fathers from other tribes.

We turn our backs on ourselves. We find biological relationships painful.

Through genes were found three aged great-grandchildren of Adolf Hitler's father, Alois, living in New York in 2009, after long ago fleeing Germany to escape the Nazis. Thirty-nine relatives of Hitler still alive in 2009 had agreed never to have children to extinguish the saga of Hitler.

That was eugenics. Traditional eugenicists never went so far as to reject all other factors and influences upon a person's character.

Large numbers of Germans and other European races feel as Hitler's relatives felt. We do so as the West.

So if white people or all people were to fade away, we feel the world would then have fewer wrongdoers. We do not appreciate ourselves enough to imagine the great arts and sciences, music and technologies, that would be lost without our race.

Eugenics remains, when it is reason to punish the West. Since the Holocaust, ours has become self-loathing eugenics.

Adolf Hitler

With his black hair and pointed features, Nazi dictator Adolf Hitler was no blond, square-jawed personification of the Aryan racial greatness he vaunted. He embodied Germans much less than most leaders embody the people they lead. While encouraging others to bear children, he never bore any of his own, reputedly because he knew he was no human ideal. The gesture might make him seem noble, a self-sacrificing hero, except that self-hatred is neither noble nor heroic.

Hitler's family hinted at genetic disorder. In his Austrian childhood home was a schizophrenic hunchback, his Aunt Johanna. As if there could be no end to the fierce irony that such a man should espouse racial purification was Hitler being part Jewish: racially, not religiously. Long after his death in 1945, genetic tests provided evidence of Hitler's paternal grandfather (or another close relative of his father Alois) being Jewish.

Had Adolf Hitler been subject to the same laws as other Germans, then he may well have died in the Holocaust. With Alois Hitler's birth certificate leaving his father's name blank, Adolf Hitler could not prove his paternal grandfather was not Jewish: that he was not a second-degree Jew, according to the Nuremberg race laws of 1935. To deal with the problem, the Nuremberg laws explicitly exempted Adolf Hitler.

Psychologist Alice Miller was a Polish-born Jewess who never met Hitler, but she drew upon evidence from people who had met him in her 1980 book *For Your Own Good*. As a boy, Hitler suffered at the hands of his tyrannical father Alois, who Miller theorised abused Adolf because he was tortured by the pain of being an illegitimate child from an affair between his German mother Maria Schickelgruber and a nineteen-year-old Jew named Frankenberger. Alois' pain, Miller theorised, became Adolf's.

When Austria became part of the greater German Reich, following the Anschluss in 1938, German tanks destroyed the birthplaces of Alois Hitler and Alois' mother. Adolf Hitler might have been eradicating evidence of his Jewish ancestry or of mental illness in his family, or he might have hated his tyrannical father and adulterous grandmother so much that he obliterated the places in which they were born. Miller theorised that the possibility he was part Jewish tormented Hitler throughout his life.

None of these facts or Miller's theory alleviates Hitler's guilt. They do suggest that Hitler's racism was more complicated than people assume racism to be.

Individual Jews

Adolf Hitler appears to have enjoyed many Jewish friends while living in Vienna before the Great War, in spite of other Viennese then fearing being overrun by East European Jews. Those Jewish populations that we now mourn were not so popular among East Europeans at the time.

Most historians believe Hitler's anti-Semitism arose after the Great War because he blamed Jews for Germany's calamitous defeat. He also blamed Germany's political leadership and communists.

Racism is a collective identity. It supplements, but need not replace, recognition of individuality within a race.

The Nuremberg race laws of 1935 exempted Jews militarily decorated during the Great War, including *Leutnant* Hugo Gutmann, the holder of an Iron Cross, First Class. Gutmann recommended Hitler also be awarded an Iron Cross, First Class, during that war, needing to argue strongly that a mere corporal should receive an honour normally accorded only officers. Hitler had already won the Iron Cross, Second Class, but Gutmann's recommendation helped.

The exemption from the Nuremberg race laws granted those decorated soldiers did not extend to their families. For his family's sake, Gutmann fled Nazi Germany, but Hitler approved Germany continuing to pay Gutmann his pension after he reached America in 1939.

Hitler had no maniacal hatred of Jews. He liked, respected, and treated well several individual Jews for their particular attributes, favours to him, or service to Germany.

Following Nazi Germany's annexation of what remained of Czechoslovakia in 1939, Hitler ordered the collection of Jewish items to form a museum of Jewish culture in Prague. In Hitler's European vision, Jews did not need to survive for us to learn of their culture.

Hitler's anti-Semitism was more complex than simplistic villainy. Genocide requires much more than mere racism.

German Self-Defence

Whenever people say something that we think or know to be false, it is difficult to know whether they are lying or they are sincere but mistaken in what they say, unless they admit to lying. We cannot enter their heads to see what they think. That is no more or less the case with Hitler than with anyone else.

There was, of course, no end of other acts to damn Hitler, but it is untrue of his critics to say he proudly peddled lies. He wrote in *Mein Kampf* of pursuing the truth, following a long line of European and particularly German philosophy seeking facts and truths. We no longer espouse anything Europeans and particularly Germans did.

Often accompanying the claim that Nazis lied is that Nazi anti-Semitism made Jews scapegoats for Germany's problems, but by 1939, Germany was prospering, after being a mess before Hitler came to power in 1933. The most that could be said was that Hitler accredited Germany's ability to rebuild herself anew after 1933 upon disenfranchising the Jews, and others.

Demagogues do not kill scapegoats. They leave them alive to continue being scapegoats.

Nor did Europeans (unlike Japanese) kill other races simply for considering them biologically inferior. If Nazis did not want to help Jews, they could have left the future to natural selection.

Nazi anti-Semitism was unlikely to have been a political scheme. More likely was that Nazis genuinely believed anti-Semitism to be Germany protecting herself and the rest of Europe from Jews.

Hitler might have feared future Jewish influence harming Germany. If so, he would have been right.

"We had the moral right," Heinrich Himmler, *Reichsführer* of the *Schutzstaffel*, told a hundred *Schutzstaffel* group leaders in Posen, occupied Poland, in 1943, "we had the duty to our people, to destroy this people which wanted to destroy us." The *Schutzstaffel* carried out the Holocaust.

Yet with Germany's defeat by the Allies imminent in April 1945, Himmler met with a representative of the World Jewish Congress to free four and a half thousand prisoners, half of them Jewish, from the women's concentration camp at Ravensbrück. With Germany doomed anyway, Himmler saw no reason to kill those prisoners.

Germans retained their morality, as our new-found individualism cannot comprehend. Most importantly, they retained their instincts for survival, likely thinking as much in terms of Europe and even humanity. European peoples tend to think on behalf of humanity.

The perpetrators of the Holocaust believed Europeans would all fare better without Jews, gypsies, and other immigrants in their midst. What Hitler called the Jewish problem required a final solution. Unlike other anti-Semitism, he attempted genocide.

Hitler, Himmler, and other perpetrators of the Holocaust considered themselves good: idealists trying to make the world better, while concealing their killing from the German people and destroying evidence of it before war's end. Truth might have been one thing. Wartime pragmatism was another.

Their sense of moral duty subsequently eroded much of Europe's confidence in morality and duty, slowly condemning the West to moral relativism and thus no morality. They were heroes in their heads, much as we are in our heads when we oppose racism.

Beauty

There was a time, centuries ago, that European fashion was to powder our skins whiter: the whitest shades of pale. Those powders were dangerous and we learnt not to use them, but we liked to be white.

There was nothing more beautiful than a white woman, nothing more handsome than a white man. Particularly in the colonies with the warmest of climes, white women especially carried umbrellas to shield their skin from the sun, although a touch of sun became evidence of wealth enough for exotic holidays abroad. Men wore hats.

Stepping back from our past sciences and more careful observation and analysis, skin colour and hair colour are the most visible measures of race. The Holocaust and propaganda it inspired stripped from us much of our sense of beauty in naturally white skin, not to mention blonde hair and blue eyes.

We came to call ourselves colour-blind and might even achieve it, but not about us. We darken our skins in the sun, exhorting suntanned bodies as our most beautiful of forms, until cancer risks worry us.

Our bodies are gifts from God and our forebears, which we traditionally felt morally bound to safeguard, but as did the tribes and races our forebears considered primitive, we pierce body parts our forebears kept supple and intact. Not only sailors now tattoo themselves like Polynesians.

Feeling disconnected from our forebears and from God, we make ourselves less beautiful and handsome, if not altogether ugly, misshapen, and grotesque. Tattoos and body piercings are not merely narcissistic expenses for people with too much money and nothing useful to do. They defile us, reflecting our failure to see we are beautiful.

We return to where we started. The coloureds who became Negroes when science came to fore and then became Africans when we focussed upon geographical origins are again people of colour. It makes them sound more fun than us colourless whites.

While Western beauty contests are open to all, several beauty contests around the world are reserved for particular races. Those contests are premised upon their race's beauty, heritage, and community. Races naturally find their race beautiful, but there are no beauty contests dedicated to white races.

While white people escape our skin colour (or lack of colour, if we will), some African and Indian women try to imitate the race we are trying not to be. They whiten their skin.

If someone were to cry out how beautiful those women are without whitening their skin, others of their race would smile fondly. So would we.

Critics call upon those women to find their self-respect, pleading with them to be proud of their skin tones and cherish their colours. That is to say, they should be proud of their race.

We could say the same to white people. There is beauty in blue-water eyes. There is splendour in silken white skin, in a woman like a white English rose.

Racial Difference

Pursuing the truth pursues evidence, but without a sense of inquiry, people do not let evidence change their opinions. Instead, they construe evidence in such a way as to verify their opinions.

If we insist people are the same, we see only similarities. Having decided to see only similarities between people, we insist people are the same in spite of any number of differences between them.

If we are open to the possibility of people being different, we see differences. Those are the differences we are supposed to celebrate when we celebrate diversity.

By celebrating diversity, we tacitly acknowledge race. Something must differ for there to be diversity.

The differences we do not specify, but we are not so racist as to consider what they are and whether they matter. We dismiss them for being inconsequential or trivialise them beyond recognition, in spite of us celebrating them.

If we pause to think what either of them means, we would see human sameness and racial difference. If that means anything, it is because we have human nature with racial traits, as was abundantly clear before the Holocaust.

Perhaps, with a little nudging, when the facts are overwhelming but unimportant, we might reluctantly admit to there being racial traits. Trying hard not to make racial inquiries, we reduce race to skin colour: shades of black, brown, olive, red, yellow, and white. We still try our darnedest not to notice it.

Bravely, we might admit races are manifest in colours and textures of hair. We dare not think as far as eye folds, bone structures, nose shapes, or the distribution of fat across faces, all of which vary between races. Those myriad of physical differences gave rise to race in the first place. It was never only skin colour.

Physical differences between races include those our naked eyes cannot see. O is the most common blood group among European races. A and AB groups are more common among some Asian races.

We confuse racially charged wrongs of the past with knowledge about race altogether, but if we could satisfy ourselves there would be no more Jewish Holocausts, at least committed by us, we could again open our minds to consider carefully what facts might be. Differences between countries and cultures are reasons to wonder whether there might be biological differences between races. Every physical, mental, and psychological feature that varies in frequency or degree between individuals might also vary between races.

Through our Age of Enlightenment, we developed a wealth of scientific theories and knowledge about race, relating to physical features, intellect, psyche, and even soul. People did not need to be scientists to recognise different temperaments between races.

Today, we talk of seeing the person instead of the race, but the person is the race. Other races notice the physical and psychological differences between races.

So, occasionally, do we. Racial differences that supposedly do not exist if they hint at reasons for the West not to welcome immigrants become a reason for criticising white people when we do not adapt to them.

Among the psychological differences between races, Asians succeed in industries in which hard work and careful research make small incremental improvements, such as electronics and manufacturing, but fail in those industries requiring imagination, intuition, and inventive leaps into the unknown, such as pharmaceutical industries and the information technologies. The West excels in both, when allowed to excel.

Racial Generalisations

Our new rules of race are complex. They require us to laud other races, but without labelling them with characteristics that explain why we laud them.

We reject racial generalisations, not because our representative samples are too small or because those generalisations may not be true in every instant. We refuse to countenance racial generalisations even when they are true in every instant.

We treat race in ways unlike our treatment of anything else. With our experiences and other knowledge, we are willing to make all manner of generalisations about people and even their physical and mental differences, categorising them as we like, provided our generalisations and categorisations do not touch upon race.

Away from race, religion, and for the most part gender, it is open slather for generalisations and stereotypes. People's work, wealth, and values, even the products they buy, can all be subjects of our ideologically acceptable generalisations. Our generalisations might be factual, but facts about race do not justify racism.

There are none of the disclaimers applied to research about people unrelated to race we apply to dismiss research with implications for race. Such research is not considered offensive or divisive, or rejected for considering matters we know to be irrelevant. Nobody finds the exception to prove it is all nonsense.

Fearful of promoting racism among people not as clever as we are, we are careful what we measure. We prohibit the possibility of a natural correlation between race and anything else, as if that were our decision to make.

There does not need to be anything derogatory in what someone theorises about races for us to object. Even neutral generalisations speak to something about race.

About matters of race, we cannot so much as wonder. Ideologies crush the notion of race.

There is to be no classification of people by race: no attempts to consider what attributes might attach to particular races. There are not to be any racial truisms or traits, because there are not to be races.

Anti-Racial Generalisations

On the other hand, we make positive generalisations about other races aplenty. We allow negative generalisations about white people. For all our individualism, we stereotype white people.

The generalisations need not be factual. They are most useful when they are not factual, helping to combat white racism.

No number of good experiences warrants positive generalisations about white people. They are reasons to like all people.

Conversely, no number of bad experiences (whether ours or anyone else's) warrants negative generalisations about other races. They are reasons to dislike all people.

The risk of truth behind such generalisations is no excuse. It intensifies our need to reject them.

We imagine racial diversity teaching us about other races, but refuse to make negative generalisations about them. We are not in the slightest bit interested in prejudiced perspectives.

Conversely, we do not need any experiences to make positive generalisations about other races. Those other races agree.

No number of exceptions affects our positive generalisations about other races. Just one exception helps us comprehensively demolish negative generalisations about other races. It is like dismissing the crimes of the Nazis because Oskar Schindler was good.

We infer good things about other races from the best of them, but not bad things from the rest of them. We base our ideals upon the best of exceptions before believing there are any bad norms, and then insist the best of exceptions are norms.

To avoid the charge of bigotry, it is not enough to make other races and cultures better than ours. We have to maintain them in perfect esteem.

We end up not knowing anything. What we think we know is not true.

Worse than mere ignorance, we are determined to see only the good in other races and disregard the bad, ending up with absurdly jaundiced views about them. Anyone wanting to know something about another race had better not ask a white person. Asking someone from a third race would be best.

Institutional White Racism

Having rejected inherited characteristics in people, we reject biological components to human thoughts and behaviour. We reject biological differences between people.

Unwaveringly resolute that all people are the same, we attribute differences between countries and peoples to something other than race, such as political and economic systems, education, and weather. Thus we insist that all races in the same environment left free will perform equally. Plainly they do not.

When the evidence commands us to acknowledge racial differences, they are not as biological facts but as political and social constructions. Rather than believing race leads to racism, we believe racism leads to race.

In our ideological vision, racial differences do not cause racism. Racism causes racial differences. Race is real because racism is.

We study not race but racism. We think we eliminate race by eliminating racism.

Certain as we are that races are not biologically real, or that all races are equal, our last explanation for particular races living in Western countries remaining disproportionately poor, unemployed, imprisoned, violent, uneducated, incompetent, unhealthy, or anything else undesirable is white people's racism of some form or another. Having eliminated overt white racism and without any sense of biological or other superiority, institutional white racism is a subliminal racism that white people do not intend or even realise but we believe we have anyway.

We assume equality is justice, as if the universe is innately fair. Thus difference becomes injustice.

Employing white people because we can do jobs becomes white privilege. Not employing other races because they cannot do those jobs becomes institutional racism, keeping other races down.

Institutional white racism can be any law, structure, programme, or anything else by which races remain unequal. The only evidence it exists are the disparities between races, but those disparities are unmistakeable.

Ours is a neat, self-fulfilling circle of logic, for people doggedly insisting races are not real or are equal. Racial disparities are evidence of institutional white racism. Institutional white racism explains racial disparities.

The lack of other evidence of our racism is not a problem. It simply proves how extensive and intrinsic our inadvertent racism must be.

For as long as we refuse to consider that races are not the same, or that races cannot prosper in close proximity to each other, we will continue tying ourselves up about everything we do. So-called institutional white racism is our failure to overcome race, in spite of our best efforts to do so. We fret about racism that does not exist, and disregard races that do.

Nature is racial. Reality is racist. Racism flows inevitably from race.

Institutional White Indulgence

When studies suggest differences between races, we do not draw conclusions about race. We draw conclusions about the studies: that they are flawed; that they are wrong.

We most aggressively dismiss evidence suggesting we are more intelligent, skilled, or otherwise better than other races. Where school or employment test results reveal racial differences, we reconstruct the syllabuses and examinations trying to obliterate those differences.

Pursuing knowledge about different races requires data without racial bias, but we do not want knowledge. We want equality. We thus introduce racial bias trying to negate racial differences.

In another reverse twist of logic so characteristic of our ideological West, we only believe intelligence and employment tests are without racial bias when they affirm the racial equality we already believe. We cannot be satisfied we have eradicated racism until rates of everything are the same across races: we are identical.

That the data continues to point to racial differences in spite of the bias we impose against those differences only indicates how significant racial differences are. The only factor more significant than race is our determination to suppress it. We thus instil more bias against us.

If immigrant races fail because we fail to accommodate them, then maybe we should cease interracial immigration until we get everything right? The best performing education systems in the world are those in racially homogenous countries, although not all racially homogenous countries perform better than racially diverse countries, not with some races.

We do not think so much about the successes and failings of immigrant races relative to each other but only relative to us, when they are faring worse than we are. We do not credit our success to our intellect and hard work, but we credit Jewish and Asian success to their intellect and hard work, without belittling their achievements by attributing those achievements to institutional racism. They agree.

None of the disclaimers we apply to dismiss talk of Africans being intellectually inferior to us we apply to talk of them being physically superior to us. We do not judge Africans by fields in which we are better than they are but fields in which we are apparently worse, most notably certain sports.

If it all seems like institutional white racism then it is, but it is racism we stubbornly cast against us. If we reached the same conclusions about boxing and basketball that we do about education and employment, we would restructure sporting programmes and contests to advantage white people.

Being true only makes the racism worse. There is no systemic oppression by white people of other races. There is systemic indulgence.

Critical Race Theory

Originating in the 1980s from black student protests at Harvard University, Critical Race Theory encompasses claims of institutional white racism and other supposed white supremacy in Western countries. It is the analytical framework by which other races blame white people for their failings and for them not getting all they want.

Critical Race Theory tries to make racial conflict sound intellectual, but it is simply another means of absolving other races of any lingering responsibility for their shortcomings. It manipulates white people into indulging other races still further and providing still more for them. It shames us into submitting even further to other races.

Nobody espouses Critical Race Theory in countries outside the West. Dominant races there do not let minority races push them around. Minority races generally know not to try.

That other races espouse Critical Race Theory in the West reflects those other races advancing their racial interests: their tribal interests. That white people should espouse it, or refuse to refute it, reflects our refusal to defend our racial interests: our separation from our race, our tribe.

Critical Race Theory might claim to be theory, but its proponents treat it as true. It is ideology, masquerading as truth as ideologies do.

That is not to say that the advocates of Critical Race Theory cannot sometimes stumble upon ideas that are true. It is simply that the facts are less important than racial objectives.

The gestures by white governments, courts, and other authorities that advance other races are probably just those white authorities advancing their sectional interests, albeit at the expense of their race. Aiding Africans in America in the 1950s and '60s might have been courting favour among African countries during the Cold War. Certainly, white authorities frequently see votes, money, and other favour for themselves in the benefits they grant other races at the expense of their own.

A more truthful Critical Race Analysis would recognise that white people's loss of our racial connectedness – our racism and other tribalism – has aided and continues to aid other races. It does so at the cost of powerless white people, as eventually all white people become.

Rational Racism

Particular variances between races might be more, less, or the same as those within races. They might be statistically significant and still mean nothing at all. If we knew what they were, we could decide whether to take them into account. They might be important.

I generalise about white people knowing that I am often referring only to the economically powerful and politically doctrinaire, but they are the ones who speak loudest. They are often the only ones speaking at all. They purport to represent white people and do. Other wealthy white people used to be more like me than they are now.

Generalisations have their limitations, but can still be true. Without generalisations, we make learning more difficult.

Stereotypes arise because people notice something often enough. There could be a thousand racial stereotypes soundly grounded in reality or none, but still they are starting points for what more we can study. In our aversion to prejudice, we miss our chance to learn, to better ourselves and others as our nineteenth-century and other forebears did.

Our refusal to consider whether human beings have something called race, let alone learn what race might mean, is wilful ignorance foisted upon us and that we foist upon each other. A lot of ignorance and presumption brought the West to where we are now.

Depending upon the details and context, racism might or might not be rational, given the evidence. Certainly irrational is the West's worsening refusal since the Holocaust even to entertain a suggestion that race could be biologically real, with psychological, mental, and important physical differences between races. Racism is never as irrational as is the West's fanatical rejection of racism.

If we wanted a scientific treatment of phobias, we could argue that our fears of race and white racism are so plainly irrational that our mental illness is race-phobia. Indifferent or oblivious to reality, we are at war against knowledge.

Animal Individualism

"We shall never be rough or heartless where it is not necessary; that is clear," said Heinrich Himmler in Posen in 1943. "We Germans, who are the only people in the world who have a decent attitude to animals, will also adopt a decent attitude to these human animals."

Himmler was instructing the perpetrators of the Holocaust to avoid unnecessary suffering by the Jews and others they killed. Apart from being an intriguing construction of what a decent attitude could be, Himmler's words blurred the distinction between humans and animals.

Having discarded our racial identities since then, there is no end of biological identities the tribeless West can discard. We no longer want race (least of all our own) and, bogged down with abstraction, are not too sure about species (least of all our own).

Individualism progressed beyond humans with Jewish philosopher Peter Singer, whose parents fled Vienna following Nazi Germany's annexation of Austria before he was born. He redefined persons so that they need not be limited to humans, provided they have individuality, consciousness, and self-awareness.

The so-called animal liberation movement belittles birth to a circumstance, which we did when we rejected race. We are not fundamentally what we are because we came into being as we are, but quite apart from the being we were born. It is as if we were all once spirits queued up waiting to be born. This one became a Yorkshireman. The next became a flea.

Western individualism has no logical boundaries in biology but only in being individuals. Replacing biology with ideology means we replace one line of discrimination with another.

Singer categorised animals as non-human persons. He categorised disabled children and old people as human non-persons. Animal rights ideology arose not from a love of animals, but from contempt for people.

In 2011, ethicists Alberto Giubilini and Francesca Minerva defined a person "to mean an individual who is capable of attributing to her own existence some (at least) basic value such that being deprived of this existence represents a loss to her." Thus we should be free to kill newborn human babies.

We were never more callous than we have become since we rejected our racism, because our rejection of racism was not a rejection of cruelty. We just moved the markers by which we are willing to kill.

Speciesism

Equating people to animals has not meant treating animals better. It means treating human beings worse.

Upholding the sanctity of human life any more than other life is speciesism: a term coined by British psychologist Richard Ryder in 1973. He equated it to racism and sexism, based on physical differences he considered to be irrelevant.

We do not excuse racism because of the behaviour of other races. Animal rights activists do not excuse speciesism because of the behaviour of other species.

Speciesism and racism become different degrees of discrimination. Racism is to speciesism as race is to species. Our Western rejection of race logically makes species untenable.

In 2005, Ryder introduced a new moral measure he called painism: there should be no discrimination against anything capable of feeling pain. We should only discriminate against "rocks and rivers and houses."

Using pain as a measure is no less arbitrary than anything else. The tribeless West already ascribes sensitivities to maggots and plants that might not feel pain. Why need a being be alive?

If speciesism is based upon physical differences and physical differences are irrelevant, then so is a division into life forms based on carbon and derived from amino acids. A plant in the garden is no less alive than a virus in the blood.

By the rest of our reasoning, viruses and bacteria should have the same rights as the simplest of animals and most disabled of human beings. Saving a person from infection can mean killing virus and bacteria, but might those virus and bacteria have as much rights to infect our bodies as we have to occupy our bodies? Anything else would be discriminatory.

We become cohabitants of our bodies. Viruses might kill us, but we prefer to die than discriminate.

Rejecting speciesism requires us to be cannibals, vegetarians, or starving. The only boundaries about which we are certain are those around our individual selves. Even those come to fade.

Replacing the arbitrariness of biological definitions of people with the arbitrariness of ideological definitions does not make life easier for other races and species. It makes ours more precarious.

The Need for Definition

Embracing the world does not end our need for identity. There remains our deepest desire for something to define us from others.

Short of surrendering all identity and dying immediately, we cannot help but discriminate. Somewhere between the thoughts deep in our heads and the atoms at the far end of the furthest galaxy, we need some point of definition. We need something to distinguish what we are from whatever we are not, in death and in life. We cannot exist without boundaries between what each of us are and what each of us are not, if we are not to disappear into a void of nothingness.

Wherever a person draws lines to say he or she identifies more with those within than without, there is arbitrariness. There is no end to the arbitrariness until all matter and space in the universe is exhausted. Even the division with God becomes arbitrary. Only atheists save themselves from that conundrum, for now.

To try to overcome that arbitrariness, we could have regard to what is natural, respecting human nature instead of trying to change it. We could reflect upon what satisfies and what does not satisfy. We could contemplate the beliefs that prosper and those that fail. We could accept our innate delineations between beings.

To that end, we could consider what people of other races believe. They continue identifying as human beings distinct from other animals. They continue identifying as races distinct from other races.

If speciesism is morally equivalent to racism, so distinguishing ourselves from other species is like distinguishing ourselves from other races, then distinguishing ourselves from other races is not so bad. If we equate racism with speciesism and speciesism is rational, then racism is rational.

Plant and Animal Discrimination

In spite of our growing rejection of speciesism, humanising animals has not led us to sense in ourselves the instincts to herd that we respect in animals. Equating humans to animals has its limits. We remain the tribeless West.

We contrast apes with humans, but do not contrast different races of humans. We examine differences between species of apes, but not between races of humans.

The West's increasing keenness to end discrimination between humans and animals might mean we stop comparing different species of apes. It might mean we resume comparing different races of humans.

When the West rejected racism, we rejected eugenics, but only for people. We are not reticent about applying eugenics to crops, plants, and animals.

When Western sciences sought knowledge, we categorised varieties of fauna and flora into species, subspecies, and genus, without anyone suggesting that was to oppress celery. While we continue to dwell upon the differences between plants to denote each of them a species, we have discarded the differences between races of people to deem human beings never anything less than a species.

Species of cats, dogs, and anything else are much like races of people. We have as much reason to respect or discard the differences between beagles and poodles as we do between races of people.

If there is confusion in language then the phrase "human race" created it. We could instead speak of a human species, whereby races are subspecies within it.

Better still, we could simply say humans. Applying the same semantics to humans that we apply to flora and fauna, we would speak of races and ethnicities of people as species and subspecies.

With plants and animals, we vent our nativist natures we can no longer express about people. With racism came nationalism, but we have become very nationalistic with our plants and animals.

Our countries exist for them, as they no longer exist for us. We assert national sovereignty not to curtail immigration, but to protect animals. We ban invasive alien species of animal, but not races of people.

With trees, we are parochial, as we find unacceptable in people. Dismissing diversity, we demand native vegetation: floral discrimination, a sort of arboreal nativism, floral racism, favouring the locals.

Environmental compatibility is not enough. Being beautiful, elegant, and even practical are immaterial. We are willing to expunge immigrant trees.

When the tribeless West wants to save a species, it is a species of plant, bird, or animal. If we really wanted to save the world, we would save ourselves.

Pets

The most profound distinction between our attitudes to animals and humans is our reticence, so far, to impose ideologies of equality and inclusion upon animals. We are free to generalise about the minds and behaviours of particular species and breeds of animals, as we are forbidden from doing about races of people.

Most often, we generalise about the capacities and temperaments of different species of dogs, the cross-breeds being the worst. Caring nothing for the pedigree of people, pet owners prefer pedigree pets to mongrels.

We struggle when domesticated animals revert to their natural instincts. We struggle when humans do, too.

The differences between humans and animals are most obvious not in matters of hate but in matters of love. Pets respond to sentiment with sentiment, remaining with us for food and shelter, while we pretend to relate with them, even to love and be loved by them. Pets can be the illusion of relationship and even adoration without commitment, challenge, or anything being said we do not want to hear.

Pets appeal to the longings of people frightened of being alone. Lonely owners concoct conversations with creatures that cannot understand.

Leaving us free of the responsibilities that loving humans can bring, pets can be bought at a whim and ask little of us. They preserve our centres of small universes another person might unsettle; pets are friends for people no longer relating to people. If we tire of them, as we tire of most things, we can sell them, give them away, or abandon them by a river.

As often as not, we would sooner abandon other people by a river than abandon our pets. Our affection for pets makes people superfluous.

In our desire to protect animals, the value we ascribe animals became not just the equal of humans. It exceeds it. Our rejection of our species reflects our rejection of our race.

Tribes without Race

During breaks in filming the 1968 American film *Planet of the Apes*, human actors congregated in the species of ape they had been made up to represent: gorillas with gorillas, chimpanzees with chimpanzees, and so forth. There was no requirement for them to do so. They did so naturally.

Tribalism is natural. Western individualism is unnatural, multiracialism even more so.

Dismissing biological linkages between people means deciding we are not born to identity. The end of our racial identities left us needing to find new identities; our tribal instincts remain.

Without race, white people imagine defining ourselves by our actions. Identities we can change are not really identities.

In place of race in the West have arisen post-racial identities we imagine melding us with other races. They do not. They divide us from our own.

Paradoxically, our individualism creates new divisions between people. We ended divisions with other races by creating new divisions within ours, creating new conflicts more personal and pervasive, intrinsic to our homes and neighbourhoods, than conflicts between races or religions ever were.

Racism once brought upper, middle, and lower classes of people into some degree of co-operation with each other, although divisions remained. Communism rejected racism because it wanted classes in conflict.

Classes become economic and social tribalism, whenever people pool their sectional interests against the national good. Without race uniting is, we have become more riddled than ever by class.

Without race, we lack real identity. Other identities are superficial by comparison.

Without race and other biological linkages, we have no real tribes. Tribes through which others and we can pass are not really tribes. They are variations on being individuals.

Our tribes without race are a string of descriptions we call identities, none of which mean as much as our insistence that race and religion not be among them. Descriptions are not identities unless they define us. Losing identity is reason to place a gun to our heads, as losing a description is not.

Work, Wealth, and Values

We used to work, spend, and opine without them being our identities. Western races were unified when our races defined us, when work, wealth, and values meant less than they have come to mean.

Instead of defining people by their race or religion, Marxism defined people by their work, wealth, and values; their values being their devotion or not to Marxism. We have come to do the same, with increasing interest in Marxism.

We try to satisfy our tribal instincts by identifying with others sharing our work, wealth, and values. They are socially acceptable discriminations by which we categorise others and ourselves, labelling people, as no other race would subscribe.

Ours are the roles that commerce and politics accord us, now that we have nothing else: the work that we do, products we buy (even clothes that we wear), and beliefs that we hold. Especially important in this Age of Ideology are values: beliefs are our most pervasive post-racial identities.

People of other races commune with their race whatever they believe. White people only commune with others of our race with whom we share political and other values, although we try our best to commune with people of other races whatever they believe.

While proudly developing the capacity to befriend a person without regard to race or religion, we have lost the ability to befriend people whatever their political opinions. We hate white people who have never or would never hurt anyone because we disagree with them, although we do not hate people from other races with whom we disagree. We never hate them.

Many of the criticisms we lay upon each other are accurate, but nobody listens. Nobody learns, too busy bickering.

We would have greater freedom to learn if our tribes did not depend upon us keeping opinions. Treating each issue on its merits, we could dispense with what fails and with what once succeeded but no longer does.

Unwilling to lose the only tribe we possess, many of us never try. Our ideals are the identities we are not brave enough to amend.

We can more easily move along when our identity does not depend upon what we or anyone else happens to do, earn, or think. If anything is a social construct, it is money, politics, and paperwork. In the darkness of our minds, they do not mean very much.

Away from the work that we do, purchases we make, or political points we score, we are alone. Vocational, economic, and political identities are for people without racial identities. Who we are is more important than anything we will ever do, own, or believe.

Who we are means being more than an individual. It means being part of a family, clan, ethnicity, and race.

Age

Allocating roles to the best and most efficient providers among the tribe was the traditional village model. Natural societies worked very well.

The fittest provided labour. The able-bodied young hunted animals, gathered food, and defended the family, village, and people. We venerated the vitality and beauty of youth, knowing we once were young.

The wisest were teachers. Elders taught, without preventing the young from prompting innovation. We revered the wisdom and experience of age, hoping eventually to become old ourselves.

Among our Western post-racial identities is defining people by age. Becoming disengaged from their parents, teenagers came into being in the 1950s.

Generations are vague, much vaguer than race. Years of birth are artificial (they really are social constructs, as we now say about race), but we take a great deal more interest in our generation than our family or race because we think our generation describes us. Generations share major social, economic, and political experiences, as well as education, music, and television. We make informed choices, but the information changes.

Generalisations by people's age and dates of birth are a new Western norm in a way that racial and religious generalisations no longer are. We generalise about older people's misbeliefs and younger people's misbehaviours as we no longer generalise about other races' misbehaviours and other religions' misbeliefs.

Our ideologies of inclusion we apply to other races and religions we do not apply to our race. We insist we are happy being around other races and religions, but unashamedly dodge the elderly and young among our race.

Racial and religious bigotries are unacceptable, but bigotry by age is fine. Age is a point of description and denigration in the tribeless West.

Our generational divide isolates our young as much as our old, keeping us apart. No less divisive than our other unnatural identities and tribalism, our generational identities and tribalism exclude us from other generations.

Rejecting Our Elderly

The more that each world war through the first half of the twentieth century diminished our confidence in our cultures, the more our respect for our elders diminished. When our sense of racial connectedness came apart after the Holocaust, that respect broke altogether. Western children attending school after World War II questioned adult authority as previous generations of schoolchildren had not.

When the first generation born after World War II came of age in the 1960s without confidence in their race and culture, they turned more harshly upon their elders, who had gone to bloody war and were still going to bloody war. Technologies were becoming more devastating than ever.

Since then, generation after generation in the tribeless West calls ourselves progressive because we think we represent progress, dismissing pretty well everything our silly elders think and awful forebears thought. We believe whatever our powerful political namesakes tell us is progressive because we so much need to be part of that tribe: that mass.

In our tribeless West, our young still work, but ours may be the first culture in history in which they no longer listen to the elderly. Age is no longer a reason to listen to what somebody says. It is a reason to turn away.

We are the worst kind of bigot, denigrating what we will become. Among people who have forsaken much of what is natural to us, growing old is an aspect of nature from which we cannot hide.

Dates of birth do not change. Ages do. When we worry, we worry what will happen to us when we age rather than what happens afterwards. Generations grow old together.

If the people who denigrate their elders think ahead to when they too will be old, they are so certain of the righteousness of their new way of thinking, they cannot imagine younger generations dismissing them, but younger generations do dismiss those antiquated fools. They learn to dismiss preceding generations from their preceding generation.

People wanting their children to respect them had better respect their parents, or provide sound reasons why they do not. They had better then respect their grandparents and other forebears, who are more worthy of respect than we have come to appreciate.

Other races do not denigrate their elderly. They look after them. They respect age and the wisdom implicit in age. They cherish their family and cultural traditions. People keeping their aged parents bear children, confident those children will keep them as they age. We used to be the same, when we were racist.

The respect for age that other races but ours hold dear is to their elderly own, not anyone else's. Without us respecting our elderly, nobody does.

Rejecting Our Young

Following from our conflict with past generations is our conflict with future generations. The older we are, the less we want to be seen to be old (worse than age is agedness in the unnatural West), but our obsession with youth is merely cosmetic, in the clothes that we wear and the colours on our faces. We have no less contempt for ages younger than ours than we have for ages older than ours. Living so much in a moment, we forget what we said, thought, and did when we were young.

We denigrate what we were, with instincts unmanaged and feelings unfettered. Calling adults infantile, childlike, or babies is socially acceptable derision. Not only adults but older children are hostile to younger children in our tribeless West.

We would stone to death anyone suspected of discriminating against other races, but freely ostracise our children without cause. We ban parents merely for being with them. We expect to avoid them, as if we had never been children too. Perhaps those of us born after 1939 never were.

The tribeless West considers age relevant to describing criminals, without concern about any correlation between age and crime, as we no longer allow race or religion to be relevant. Youth crime becomes a euphemism for crime by races younger than we are, for white people believing young people are criminal but not believing other races are.

Other races' devotion to children is to their children, not ours. Without us protecting our children, nobody will.

No conflicts are more damaging to a people than generational conflicts. When children feeling denigrated for being children age into adults, the only people they revile more than they revile themselves and their parents are new children coming through: the unborn who could have been our futures. They thus prevent them coming into existence.

Ancestors

Parents, grandparents, and great-grandparents are steps along biological chains. Our forebears offer us long families much fuller than the fickle small families passing through our fleeting small lives. They offer us forever.

Common ancestors we have no idea who were connect us with people alive today we have never before met, never before known existed. Shared ancestries bring people together, if we let them.

We are family, but when biological descriptions of people became incidental, so did biological relationships between them. Marxism and the tribeless West dismiss any significance for both biological descriptions and biological relationships as being merely human constructions.

If we must allude to race but always disavowing race as much as we can, we refer to race by any other term we can conjure. We might make vague expressions of people's pasts that other races call race: race without race.

Every time we speak of a person's ancestry and descent to avoid mention of race, we affirm how racist biological links through generations are. Rejecting racism makes identifying with our ancestors untenable.

Without race, we are without people preceding us: without roots. No longer identifying with our ancestors means we no longer sense being perennial families. No longer do we count generations long dead as being us. We feel no bloodlines.

All the races on earth honour their ancestors, but ours. We honour other people's ancestors, but rarely our own. We dishonour our dead, those names born one day to die, but if we do not remember our ancestors, then nobody will.

Families

What remains without race is the Western notion of a nuclear family: those people living in the house with us, affecting us or not, interacting with us or not. Rejecting biological linkages between people makes our nuclear families no more tenable than our ancestral families.

Families, like races, are biological relationships. To believe we are only individual selves, individualism, we discard biological relations between people: race, family, and parenthood. We ignore biological connectedness between parents and children, and the relationship between each mother and father that their child creates.

Biological intimacy falls away. Biological relationship disappears. Rejecting one biological relationship became rejecting them all.

Without racial loyalties we have no biological loyalties and so no family loyalties. The end of white racism correlates with the breakdown of white families. Ending race ends families.

For as long as families are racially homogenous, as families once were, families are racist. They are racist even if they are multiracial, for being primarily of one race or two and for the races they are not.

Relationships, such as survive, are between pairs of individuals, who may or may not be related. We are unfettered individuals, like the rest of our household.

Individualism is our separation from others. Individualism is intrinsically incompatible with families.

There is no family structure in the tribeless West. There are no social structures among individuals.

We recognise the damage that individualism does to families, but only other races' families. We defend those families as we do not defend our families.

Racists do not focus upon being individuals at the expense of their people. Thus racists are much less likely than individualists to abandon their families, even if they abandon those among their family members who abandon them.

We do not begrudge other races their racial and familial identities. Seeing boundaries around their clans and traditional tribes, some find lesser boundaries around their religion.

Without the poison of individualism, retaining their biological connections means retaining their racial and family connections. Their connectedness with their race is connectedness with their family. Retaining their racial ethos means retaining their family ethos. They feel their families. They revel in race.

People identifying with their race identify with their families. The togetherness of family is the togetherness of race. Family and race are belonging.

Connections with our furthest relatives could spread our families too. From being families united by blood, flesh, and bones, we become clans united by blood, flesh, and bones.

If identifying with our family is morally right, then so is identifying with our clan. Soon enough, so is identifying with our race. Families reach into races, so that loving our family means loving our race, which is what scares us so much about families.

Metaphorical Families

Family would have remained a racist concept had we retained its biological definition, but even our lowly nuclear families have lost sense of blood and other biology in the tribeless West. We without sense of biological relationships dismiss biological families as merely social and political constructions.

Instead of helping families, we carry out esoteric debates about what constitutes a family. We worry more about people without families feeling better than we worry about weakening family bonds.

Where biological relationship does not matter, families are whatever we want families to be. We call any two or more people a family even if they are unaware of each other, if we feel better doing so.

We might speak of being a family for no other reason than there is money involved. Companies will tell us that all we who purchase their products are a family. Lonely people believe them.

In our desperation to avoid war and holocaust after 1945, the tribeless West constructed our grandest of all metaphors: the single world family. Embracing everyone, we without families call everyone our family. We without siblings say we have billions of them.

Being Western, we are at the head of our imaginary world family, responsible for aiding our charges. It is our white parents' burden.

Deeming our biological families the equals of a family in Swaziland might make us more generous to the people of Swaziland, but it leaves us neglecting our biological families. The result is ambivalence to the people around us.

Other races still let genetic disposition determine families. For all the Swazis' poverty and poor education, their families live for them.

Our families do not live for us. Strangers we have never met in lands we have never entered are our moral equivalent of people whose blood we share, and a hedgehog hiding in the shrubbery.

Therein lies our aloneness. Thinking we are related to everyone leaves us feeling we are not related to anyone.

Caring about all people becomes conceit by people caring for none. People trying to love everyone love no one.

Ours is family without families. We are the people unloved while our families aid other races, so proudly disloyal to their kin.

Believing metaphors are real and whatever makes us happy, we lost ourselves in the metaphor. It would be nice if white people insisting they love people loved their real families, even if that meant caring a little less about strangers.

Love and Discrimination

Love and friendship command loyalty. When we love, we discriminate.

Discrimination need not harm others. It can simply assist one's own.

We in the tribeless West do not just refuse to discriminate in favour of our compatriots' families. We refuse to discriminate in favour of our families.

Nepotism is another natural discrimination we deride that other races proudly practice. "I and my brother against my cousin," says one Arab proverb. "I, my brother, and my cousin against the outsider."

Human nature is to defend one's tribe and family. When conflict arises, people of other races draw support from their near and distant relatives. We barely know ours.

Convinced we cannot differentiate, we leave our relatives helpless. Convinced they cannot differentiate, our relatives leave us helpless.

At the heart of our solitude is our refusal to discriminate for our relatives while other races discriminate for theirs. We commoditise our kin along with all other commodity people.

We disavow family loyalties however good our relatives are. Other races maintain their family loyalties however bad their relatives are.

Western individualism discounts family and friends. At best, we equate our families to strangers' families. Anything else would be discriminatory.

At worst, we subordinate our families to strangers' families. Sometimes, it would be nice enough if our families did not discriminate *against* us.

In this Age of Ideology, we make subjective thoughts more important than our blood relations beside us. Treating the rest of our family as we treat the rest of our race, we submit our relatives to our judgements as we do not submit people from other races.

Any familial affection we feel depends upon what our relatives think and do, although the politics we prefer are not our people's interests. Our ideologies are other people's interests: our rejection of our race and collective religion. Our loyalties are to other people's families.

Without discrimination, there is no love. When we made discrimination to help our family seem a fault, we made loving our family a fault.

If we accept discriminating for our children's benefit, we accept discriminating to benefit our siblings, parents, grandparents, cousins, aunts, uncles, and so forth. Family prevails over friends, however far a family might reach. It thus follows our families' lives are worth more to us than other lives on earth. Distant relatives are our clans. Our most distant relatives are our races.

Without our families and races standing by us in our tribeless West, nobody else has reason to do so. No one is on our side, loving us, not even us. It is the heart of our despair.

Our Children

Through the millennia and more that ideally our families endure, the most important generation is not the last. It is the next.

Raising children might not teach people much about being a parent, but it teaches us how little we know. Thus nothing teaches us more about our parents than being parents too, leading us to judge them more harshly or softly. Treating our children as the most important people on earth can end our last esteem for parents who did not place us first in their lives, or even second, third, or fourth.

Becoming parents, we do the best we can with what we know. We try not to make the same mistakes our parents made. We make new mistakes.

I try to take the good aspects of my childhood, parents' actions, and rest of my experiences and replicate them for my children. I try to avoid repeating the bad aspects of my past for my children, and for me.

All we really know to teach our children is to learn. At this time in our histories, they should not be like us.

Individualist children become individualist parents. Parental individualism means our only reasons to be parents are our children's relationships with us, when we are in the mood. Our interest in our children is for their immediate impact upon us.

Proudly we prefer to pursue our personal causes and careers, while we condemn our children to faring alone in the world. Treating our possessions as ours alone, Western parents refuse to imagine sharing ownership of their possessions with their spouse and children any more than with their race.

Parents of other races help their children to degrees that Western parents refuse. Rich Asians, Africans, and Arabs defend not just their tribes' and races' wealth but their family wealth too, building dynasties. Their future generations will command societies, because of the wombs from which they come.

Mothers normally forge family units, but white parents have become individuals. White women used to be the most insistent that other white women expend time away from work caring for their children. They have become the most insistent that other white women do not. Seeing and holding our children are not important.

Conversely, white women expending their lives caring for other races' children can expect to be admired by other white people. How happy a people might white people be to know our families cared so much for us?

The tribeless West finds loving so difficult, but if we want our children to love us, we need to love them. Our generations feeling unloved by their parents do not love them in return. They do not love their forebears. They do not love themselves.

Parenting is not so difficult. It requires loving our children and demonstrating it as best as we can. Our unconditional love teaches our children to love themselves unconditionally or would, if nothing else gets in the way.

It is self-evident to say, but the only biological family of which we can be part is our own. Children make spouses a family, joining two families. Looking up to us, they make us smile, if we give them the chance. We smile because of them, if we give ourselves the chance.

With senses of family, any tribe to which we belong, we belong with our forebears, spouses, children, and grandchildren. Our family's history and future are ours; biology joins us to our forebears and descendants. Like races, we are never alone.

Pride lies not in anything we do but what we are: a family. Nothing any of us do in our work or studies lets our families down. We only let our families down by the ways we treat each other. Caring about lives beyond our own, we defend our descendants from harm.

Other People's Children

Coins in glass jars and automatic debits from credit cards and bank accounts are not parenthood. They are charity.

Adoption is not childbearing. It is child acquiring. Adoption is not reproduction or procreation.

The West has a long record of infertile couples adopting babies, carefully matching their race and religion. People did not pretend that adopters and step-parents were parents or pretend that adoptees and step-children were their children. Parenthood was biological, nothing else.

We lost interest in race and religion. We adopt anyone.

Families having become more metaphorical than real in the tribeless West, there is only a small step to metaphorical parenthood. Without genetic relationship to consider, we equate adoption with parenthood, as if legal process and paperwork make a stranger somebody's child.

In a West where people choose their identities and anything can be an identity, people are parents if we identify as being parents. We without children or thought of bearing children pretend to be parents: that other people's children are ours. We have made parents indistinguishable from people in positions like parenthood: *in loco parentis*.

Conversely, we without a parent call a person acting like our mother or father our mother or father. We are their children if we identify as their children.

We are obliterating biological parenthood. Parents are all *in loco parentis*.

Adoptive parents are no longer only those unable to bear children. We might want a baby, but not want to wait the nine months of pregnancy. We might prefer the choice that comes from babies already produced to the uncertainty of speculative birth.

Outside the West, there is no talk of natural parents because the only parents are natural. There are not birth mothers and other mothers, but only mothers or not. Families and parenthood remain biological.

No race but ours contemplates adopting and fostering children from other races. Few races but ours contemplate adoption and fostering within their race. People might care for their relatives' babies, but that reflects their familial identities. Confining adoption to close relatives maintains their family lines.

Islam allows fostering of children, but bans adoption outright, safeguarding patrimony and inheritance. Egypt extended the ban to Christians, for fear Christians might adopt Muslim babies and raise them as Christian.

Interracial Adoption

Nowhere does our Western witlessness about race meet so spectacularly with our paternalistic and maternalistic attitudes to other races than in the practice of childless white people traversing every biological and cultural schism to bring home what we think are commodity children. Ending our genetic link through generations, we do not simply end our family lines. We replace them with other family lines.

In much the same way, our senses of countries move effortlessly between races, from ours to immigrant races. Without bloodline or other biology in mind, the West perceives populations oblivious to heredity and race.

We are not alleviating population pressures in the countries from which we adopt children. Those parents bear more babies to replace them.

Our global adopters might be eager and even emotionally desperate to be parents. They might want to help the poor children, presuming they are as blithely oblivious to race as we are. They might want a plaything, toy, or pet human in the house.

Whatever the motivation, it may be that few adopters wilfully mistreat their adoptees. Most ply them with material wealth and something like love, much as white Australians from 1909 until the 1970s treated mixed-race and other Aboriginal children whose indigenous parents were unable or unwilling to raise them. The danger came primarily from male Aborigines, especially when intoxicated. To protect those children, governments removed them from their people and entrusted them to caring white foster parents.

Britons, New Zealanders, Americans, and Canadians did the same through that period with neglected white and indigenous children. Americans came to call theirs the Baby Scoop Era.

Those babies and children became adults. Those of other races recognised biological links between people in family and race, in spite of us not recognising them.

Early in the twenty-first century, the West's romantic visions of other races cannot imagine people of other races neglecting their children. Our hostility to our race cannot imagine our forebears helping them. Thus, our only explanation for our forebears removing children of other races is the genocide we are certain they constantly pursued. Thus in spite of all the benefits we provided our charges, we apologise, over and over.

We are still scooping other people's children. The circumstances of foreign children today are normally much cleaner and safer than were those of indigenous children in the twentieth century but, if removing those indigenous children was so harmful to them for removing them from their families, tribes, and races, the adoption of foreign children today must also be harmful. Some of those foreign children are already complaining.

If our coming generations remain as eager to apologise to other races, there might well come a time we apologise for having adopted foreign children. Aged adopters might remark they acted with the best of intentions and government approval, treating the adopted children as if they were their own, but nobody will listen. Adopters mentioning the fine lives they afforded those foreign children or the harsh lives from which those children were saved can expect to be jeered, much as we jeer our elders saying they thought they were helping the mixed-race and indigenous children they adopted.

Nothing will diminish our descendants condemning us. They too will prostrate themselves in shame.

Mixed-Race Marriage

Traditionally, interracial and other intertribal carnal relations were normally men's spoils of war or acts of other conflict or exploitation. They were directed not just at the women of the other tribe or race, but at the other tribe or race altogether. They often still are.

Our natural instinct is to mate with our own, making intertribal marriage and consensual miscegenation unnatural. Tribes traditionally considered interracial and other intertribal marriage to be immoral for compromising the integrity of families, tribes, and races.

With little or no interracial immigration, there was no need for most countries to prohibit interracial marriage. We banned interracial relations in our colonies, as much because it exploited indigenous people as it comprised the integrity of our races and theirs.

By World War II, thirty-eight American states prohibited interracial marriage involving white people. In our determination to embrace other races after the Jewish Holocaust, American judges, not the American people, overturned those laws.

Our tribeless West plays havoc with natural instincts, but we still instinctively tend to choose spouses that look at least a little like us. White people no longer allow the similarities that we desire in our spouses to include race. Marrying within a race requires racism, much like the speciesism in not marrying chimpanzees.

Amidst our absurd anti-Western ideologies, white people preferring to marry people of other races are not racist, but those preferring to marry people of our race are. We are supposed not just to welcome other races into our neighbourhoods but to wed them.

Government sex-education and consumer advertising promote mixed-race relationships. One race of the two varies, but the other is always white.

We are not simply indifferent to our race and human nature. We are working against them.

The problems of mixed-race marriages are much like those of multiculturalism. We do not acknowledge those either.

None of us are confined to one choice of spouse. We can like and befriend the kindest, loveliest people on earth, without marrying them. We can have bed mates and even lovers from other races, without marrying them. Other races do.

If we do not value ourselves there is no reason that people of other races will value us, but some of them do. People of other races marrying white people know that we do not assert our heritage and culture. We submit to theirs. They might also recognise our genetic attributes we refuse to believe.

Mixed-Race Children

Marrying within a race allows the couple's shared heritage and culture to be a part of their family and children's lives, sharing the future as much as the past. Identity remains simple.

We traditionally saw interracial marriage as especially unfair on the mixed-race children. They suffered for not being of a race.

Colonial Europeans used to talk of indigenous people being mixed-race or half-caste, before doing so became offensive. That was too biological, scientific, and racist.

Instead of being part indigenous, people are now indigenous or not. They can decide, provided other indigenous people agree.

Whenever only one parent is white, then the other parent normally defines their children, as it did when we enjoyed our racial identities. Being white was like fresh milk that could only be soiled by adding anything else. Having lost our racial self-respect, being white became like milk to which adding flavour means we taste only the flavour.

Anyone who is not purely white is not white. The darker race defines, not just with partially white people.

Mixed-race children often lack racial identities, but white people now lack racial identities too. In a world where the primary and often only identities are racial, they often lack identities altogether.

Where families remain valued, mixed-race children are often outcasts, belonging not to two races but to none. Indians dismiss those in the Indian north-east mixed with Mongols as "chinky-eyed."

Other races question the loyalties of mixed-race offspring. We are individuals, not loyal to our race or countries, anyway.

Even in Western countries, mixed-race people find it hard to know who their people are. They might speak of feeling mixed up inside; both races might not see them as theirs. Not being of a race is to be incomplete.

They also suffer biological complications. Mixed-race people find it more challenging to identify bone marrow transplant donors with the necessary genetic match to save their lives. If there are differences in brains between races, that could suggest psychological problems for anyone mixed-race.

With racial mixing, white people disappear. Other races do not. They in their countries remain.

Unfettered individualists do not care, but pillory those who do. Some welcome our demise, our sweet self-destruction, basking in the birth of what they consider the new race replacing us.

Instead of our diminution making us think we are doing something wrong, it makes us more certain how wonderful we have become. We are smitten with our self-destruction, never so proud of being a people as we are proud of not being one.

Our new racism welcomes not just the end of our old racism but the end of our race. Genocide never contemplated races committing racial suicide, but we do not consider what we are doing genocide because we have decided we are not a race or races anyway. There is nothing to eradicate. The truth of being a people dies before a people does, leading by whatever turns and motivations to our stupid suicide.

Hitler's Individualism

In spite of so much and so many stacked against her, Germany came close to winning World War II. By early 1945, she was facing imminent defeat. Brave Germans had suffered horrors in Stalingrad and elsewhere among the impoverished, wounded, and dead men and women, but dictator Adolf Hitler turned on the German people he blamed for failing him. On the third Monday of March 1945, he ordered the destruction of what remained of German industry, communications, and transport systems.

If Hitler's Nero Decree sought to deny German infrastructure to her enemies, then it was probably because the Versailles Treaty convinced Hitler that France and other countries would again punish Germany by confiscating her infrastructure after the war. In all events, Hitler denied a future Germany the chance to retain or recover that infrastructure as Hitler had recovered much of what Germany lost at Versailles. If Hitler were to fail, Germany should be destroyed. Whatever he thought about Jews, Hitler's wrath came to want the destruction of Germany.

Hitler's war cost millions of German lives, many of them because of his egomaniacal refusal to surrender when the war was lost. He demanded Germans fight to their deaths, but he killed himself rather than suffer a fate like that of Italian dictator Benito Mussolini.

No nationalist would let his people suffer and die, as Hitler did. Nationalists might sacrifice themselves where nothing less defends their race and country, but nationalists do not kill themselves for their sakes, as Hitler did. That is individualism.

Central to Hitler's dictatorship was a personality cult. Dictatorships are generally individualist. Personality cults are always individualist.

Hitler might simply have exploited the nationalism of others in pursuit of his personal ambitions. Far from being the definitive German nationalist, Hitler might have been the definitive German individualist. With such worldwide ambitions and a willingness to send Germans into war and keep them in that war to die, he might have been the definitive German globalist.

Following Hitler

Across the West, among vanquished and victors alike, rulers came to hold their races in the same contempt as Adolf Hitler held

Germans at the end of World War II. Soon enough, so did the ruled.

Several generations after his death too slow coming, Hitler would seem to be enjoying victory, after all. The rest of Western history has gone, leaving little more than Hitler standing. He inspired a Germany, Europe, and West haunted by the ghosts of Holocaust to follow him into oblivion, succeeding destruction with our self-destruction. Our rejection of racism matters more than our race, to the end.

We confuse race with murder. So determined are we to avoid committing another Jewish Holocaust, we accept a Western Holocaust. If our prejudices lie dormant through our tolerance to be reawakened by people and circumstances inspiring us, as they awoke in tolerant Germany in the 1920s and '30s with such effect, then the world will only be rid of Western prejudice when it is rid of Western peoples, we men and women capable of Holocaust. That we died ending the Jewish Holocaust in 1945 is not enough.

The end of our race is the end of our racism. Other races will still be racist, but they have not killed Jews as we killed Jews, not recently anyway, not yet.

Completely comfortable with shaming ourselves down, we are frightened to stop. If Nazi Germany's claims of racial superiority justified the Jewish Holocaust, then our new-found reeking of racial inferiority justifies our racial suicide.

It is more than our comeuppance for a past in which we felt superior to other races. We are prisoners of war imprisoned in the camps of Auschwitz, frozen at the open gates of Birkenau upon liberation in January 1945, until we die convinced that we are finally free.

We have surrendered, and have had driven from us, every sense of self-esteem as no other race in history has suffered, much as Jews in Europe increasingly felt under Nazism. We are what the Jews had become by the time they stepped into the gas chambers, lied to at their end, promised a place better than their wartime ghettoes, only to die.

The Nazi regime lasted only twelve years. We have experienced decade after decade of this.

Restoring our self-respect is not conservatism. It is restoration: stepping out of Auschwitz-Birkenau, closing the gates behind us. It is not trivialising that most infamous of holocausts to say that considering all of our histories, we have at least as much reason as other races to enjoy self-respecting racism.

If all of us think of ourselves and our spouses and children, then that would be enough. From families, races flow.

Hitler never achieved his genocide of Jews but, more cruelly than he could have dreamed, the genocide of Germans and other European peoples is under way. To whatever extent our suicide is not of our doing but the result of other people's hands and propaganda, theirs is the worst act of genocide in history. Manipulating us to die is murder.

3. BIOLOGICAL US:
GENDER AND SEXUALITY

The most innate of human instincts is to survive: self-preservation, preserving the tribe. Nothing is more natural than a desire to defend and perpetuate our family and selves: finding mates; bearing, raising, and safeguarding our young.

Instincts to procreate naturally attract men to women and women to men in circumstances best for their children, families, and tribe. There is every reason why we would innately desire the opposite gender and none at all why we would desire our own, or desire something else altogether.

Those instincts are evolutionary psychology, but individualism does not simply reflect the West's separation from our natural instincts. It drives more separation.

Without a sense of being part of a tribe, we have no sense of that tribe surviving. We have no sense of being part of a family or race, and so no interest in our family or race surviving.

Families and races survive, when their people procreate. Their selves survive, when their selves are their families and races.

Individuals do not survive, childless or not. They are born, live, and die alone. People die, when individual selves are their only selves.

So caught up are we with being individuals in a global humanity, we have lost sight of being families to save. Without sense of being clans and races to last, we lost the premise of procreation.

Discarding our innate tribal natures separates us from our natural sexual and childbearing instincts, on which our races and families depend to endure. In the choice between ideologies of inclusion and evolutionary psychology, we dismissed human nature.

Sexual Morality

Traditionally men and women defended their children, families, and tribes, albeit in different ways. Men as hunters and warriors need not keep women from hunting and battle. Women as nurturers need not deter men from tending to their young.

Caring for men, women, and children does not mean letting people do whatever they want to do, when they act against their good or the tribal good. Morality means caring enough about people to let them know, subtly perhaps, that what they are doing is wrong, harming others among their tribespeople or themselves. Morality is paternalistic and maternalistic to be sure, but so is any other expression of people looking after each other: tribalism.

Women were the primary drivers setting social mores and moulding morality for the good of them all, with their recognition that nothing was more important for a community than raising their children in secure and stable families and clans. Sexual morality protected women, often from other women poaching their men: the fathers of their children. Women relied upon men to keep and protect them through their pregnancies and raising their children.

Socially, women were the most powerful of people. For women, men provided not just love, food, and shelter, but chivalry: sovereignty. Men were the lawmakers, who enforced through civil and criminal laws those social mores that women developed and enforced by other means, such as social exclusion of wrongdoers until they corrected their behaviour.

Women became the moral guardians of them all. Women and thus men condemned behaviours that harmed the tribe. They endorsed behaviours aiding the tribe: the family, nation, and race.

Extra-Marital Relations

If something natural is not good, then it is because something else natural is better. Maintaining the family and tribe is natural and better.

Nothing is more natural than for a man to want to bed a beautiful woman, or for a woman to want a strong man to bed her, but hers is the risk of pregnancy. Thus women developed the sexual morality by which men do not act upon their sexual instincts within the tribe and by which tribesmen and women do not sleep together outside a commitment of the kind we call marriage.

Marriage was primarily for women's and children's benefit. Men subscribed because they shared the same tribe as those women and children.

Through the twentieth century, as much for the benefit of men as for the benefit of women, contraception reduced women's risks of falling pregnant to men not of their choosing or at inconvenient times. That reduced a moral imperative behind society's prohibition on extra-marital relations, but did not alter human nature.

In our youths, my Christian friend Bruce Hanke believed that pre-marital relations constituted adultery against future spouses, but there cannot be a breach of vows before vows are made. Presumably, pre-marital relations between men and women who marry each other would not be adultery.

There might be reason in human nature for men and women not to bed each other outside marriage. Making love might really be making love, if consensual carnal relations create feelings of the kind we call love, not just at that time but thereafter, in women, men, or both.

Morality being tribal, natural feelings can be immoral for the harm they do families and tribes. Natural feelings are not immoral when only harming people outside a tribe.

Lust might be natural but still be immoral for objectifying people who should not be objectified. Safeguarding their families, women traditionally recognised promiscuity, adultery, and other sexual relations outside marriage to be immoral, especially by other women. Thus people restrain themselves for the sake of their families and tribe.

Men distinguish the many women they would bed, from the fewer women they would marry. Men prefer to marry women who are not promiscuous, but have saved their virtue for them.

Women continue to care less about their men's adventurous pasts than they care about the behaviour of other women. If we tolerate promiscuous men more than promiscuous women, it might be because promiscuous men prove their virility, but we entrust our children, families, and futures to responsible mothers.

Most, if not all, traditional societies condemned adultery for harming spouses and children. Those more tolerant of adultery were tolerant only when adultery was discreet, without publicly demeaning the spouse or belittling marriage. Promiscuous married men threatened their families only when people knew of their promiscuity, or when they left their families.

Traditionally, other women often blamed the wives for their husbands' infidelities, because they felt those wives had failed to satisfy their husbands or otherwise provide the greater reason for their husbands to be faithful to them. If that seems cruel towards those wives, it is more contemptuous towards those husbands.

Women generally continue to care less about their husbands' extra-marital affairs than men care about their wives' extra-marital affairs, provided those husbands provide for them materially and comfortably and do not humiliate them or their family structures by being indiscreet with their affairs. Marriages survive husbands' affairs better than they survive wives' affairs.

Married men do not cease recognising the beauty of women other than their wives. Their love or other commitments to their families keep them from doing anything to harm their families, or worst of all, losing those families. Families and tribes benefit people enough for maintaining them to be in their personal interests.

If tribalism does not underpin morality, then self-interest amidst a tribe does. Sometimes, people blunder.

The End of Sexual Morality

For drawing upon the wisdom and interests of many, social mores are more desirable than values formed by any one person. Societies guide people to natural norms and the morality that goes with them, but the West has societies no more. We have become only individuals.

We thus have no social mores: the foundations of morality. We have no communities from which morality can naturally form. We care for nobody else, and nobody else cares for us.

We came to consider previously immoral actions victimless, as if we could never be victims of our own actions. We ceased calling them crimes.

Behaviour we used to see as immoral for the harm it does families, children, and communities we came to accept because we personally do not suffer. Without a sense of connectedness in a tribe and thus morality, other people are no longer our concern. We do not care if children are not being born or, if they are, for their safe and secure raising. No longer are we communities of people caring for our collective future.

Without other morality, there is no sexual morality. Without sexual morality, there is no other morality. The genesis of one morality is that of the other: tribalism.

Refusing to feel part of a family, race, or other meaningfully integrated whole, we have no premise for taking interests in what others among us do, except in the course of our work. We expect others not to intrude upon us, judge us, or care about us, except in the course of their work.

Morality became unethical, if not illegal. We have no right to morality.

When immoral people decide what is moral, then they denote immorality to be morality, if only for leaving others alone. Morality becomes immorality, if only for disagreeing with them, intruding upon others.

If we were merely trying to be nice, we would tolerate morality. We do not.

Morality is not just obsolete in the West. We consider it oppressive. We have become hostile to morality for interrupting our individual way: our right to do whatever we want to do and our privilege not to care about others doing whatever they want to do, however perverse and destructive their behaviour or ours. In the tribeless West, morality became bigotry, a phobia, or hatred.

Gender Ideology

Conceitedly, we might presume that people believing our ideologies are smart enough to understand them while people rejecting them are stupid, but intelligence did not lead us to reject race, gender, and the norm of heterosexuality. Complication did. Ideologies complicated us.

Much about the world is necessarily complicated. Gender and sexuality do not need to be. We are physiologically real, with genes, chromosomes, biological gender and the desires that go with it.

Men and women are different. The differences are beautiful, so far as women are concerned. The differences are practical.

Without tribalism, natural social mores and moralities gave way to political pressures. The morality of community gave way to ideologies of indifference.

The West's initial rejection of race after World War II was a rejection of biological reality. Each step abandoning biological reality compounded into the next.

Rejecting the observable reality of race after the Jewish Holocaust means we could hardly help in time but reject the observable reality of gender. There came a new word to mean recognising natural differences between men and women: sexism, akin to racism.

Man and woman, male and female, ladies and gentlemen are all sexist delineations between people. No longer enjoying the differences between genders, we deny them.

If the genetic differences between races are inadequate for us to delineate between races, gender does not stand a chance. One gene alone might determine a person's gender. Certainly, one chromosome does.

That does not make us tolerate racism. It makes us more intolerant of sexism.

Much as it is with race, the purported science that much of Western academia feels compelled to preach about gender and sexuality is not factual. It is a political construction construing biology away, driving us into unnatural diversity. Instead of respecting biology, we defy it.

As we do with race, we dismiss the physical and psychological differences between men and women as merely human social and political constructions. We called it gender theory rather than race theory because we do not like mentioning race, but they are the same doctrines.

Gender theory or gender studies became gender ideology when people insisted it was true. If the tribeless West has a descriptor, it is gender ideology.

Ours is another view unique to the West and, to a degree, Jewry. The rest of the world believes in biology: race, gender, family, and species are facts. Race is their identity, their widest tribe; they do not need another. They get on with their lives.

For us, race, gender, and family are not facts, although gender and family are among our post-racial identities. They are just not biological.

Unconstrained by their effect upon people, our ideologies of inclusion have become increasingly complex, with chaos and contradictions. Intelligence is not a prerequisite. Obedience is the primary qualification, along with a willingness to completely disregard the evidence around us.

Imagination helps. There is no idea too preposterous for our ideological West to embrace in the name of inclusion.

In a field with nothing intellectual about it, any fool can become an expert, academic, or scholar. If a man can identify as a woman then a fool can identify as a genius.

Biological Individualism

Gender ideology is not just a rejection of biological difference. It is a rejection of biological relationship and tribalism. Gender ideology has no regard for our children, families, and races.

On the one hand, we are individuals. On the other, we are everyone. All we are not are biological tribes.

Gender ideology is individualism. Paradoxically, the political construction is not race or gender but individualism: a rejection of other people. Only a person born alone on an island without sense of another person cannot imagine gender, family, or race. Without another creature, the person has no sense of species.

Individualism is a right to aloneness, albeit equal aloneness. It is a rejection of societies and tribes.

Being fat or thin, smart or stupid, only mean something by comparison with somebody else. Individualism rejects comparisons, as if they were judgements.

We in the tribeless West might each be on our individualist islands, lonely even, but we are not fully alone. People who so effectively report the news, craft our entertainment, market products for sale, and lead our children's education apply their skills and resources to moulding our attitudes to race, gender, and sexuality.

Our schools, media, and other human authorities convince the West that liking other races, homosexuals, and the so-called transgendered is natural and normal, but that liking our race, parents, or children is neither natural nor normal. None of it is true.

To witness media, books, and other forces so quickly and cleverly change public opinion around the West, especially the young without knowledge of anything else, about matters of human biology is to conclude that propaganda can persuade a population of anything. Our Age of Ideology is predicated upon the idea.

Biological Ambiguity

Ideology rules: perfect personal liberty demands an unending ecstasy of rights to do whatever we want to do, unfettered by fact. We have come to consider reality restraining.

Facts about people became old-fashioned, human biology a dated idea. In our fixation with personal rights, facts become negative impacts, confining us from being whatever we wish to be. Ideologies treat biological facts like they are boxes, denying people their delusional liberties. In pursuit of our personal freedoms, we are supposed to be free to find what defines and refines us. We do not let facts hold us back.

We are trying to be nice, but it is hard to imagine anything more damaging to people's mental well-being than setting them apart from reality. Never mind complexities, it is the simplicities of human biology the West no longer understands.

Biological definitions are narrow, but if they were not narrow, they would not be definitions. Without them, we have no definition, vanishing in a haze of undefined norms.

Life and the universe leave enough uncertainty around us without uncertainty about our fundamental selves. We have created uncertainty at the cores of our beings where there need not be any. Without the certainty of human biology, we suffer the vagaries of ideology.

Striving so hard to be everyone, we end up being no one, foundering in our sea of insecurity. Abandoning human biology condemns us to no end of abstractions and ambiguity; never mind *who*, we do not know *what* we are.

The End of Normality

With very few exceptions through history, we are not meaningfully unique. Whatever moments of our lives, thoughts, and tastes might in combination be unique, are completely unimportant. Far more important are those aspects of our lives, thoughts, and tastes that are common to our race, gender, and age: our racial, gender, and generational traits. Generalisations they might be, but they describe us.

Ordinarily, people recognise what is natural from seeing what is normal among other people. Other races remain their tribal selves, with senses of what is normal. That is normal among everyone, among particular races and tribes, among men and among women, and among people of a particular age.

Western individualism separates us from other people. It also, from our perspective, separates other people from each other.

Preoccupied with our avowed individualism, we of the West became obsessed with thinking each of us is unique. Thus we refuse to recognise commonalities among people. We fix upon any exceptions we think we can find. No longer do we contemplate natural desires and instincts in people, as we did in our time of science and as other races still do. We lose a sense of anything being normal.

Words became nonsensical with ideology and never more nonsensical than with gender ideology. As we push our natures further away, we in the unnatural West dismiss the natural attraction between men and women as heterosexism, akin to sexism. Whenever our unnatural West labels a fact or human nature a mere "-ism," then coming close behind is labelling a belief in that fact or nature to be bigotry, a phobia, or hate speech.

Cis-heteronormative replaced talk of being normal. Normal it remained.

Our rejection of biological norms and reality leaves people vulnerable to aberrant feelings and behaviours. When sexual desires can be all over the place, we lose track of the natural function of sexuality: procreation. The West's rejection of biological gender and heterosexuality as being normal are rejections of childbearing as being normal. Like the rest of our individualism, they are rejections of being families, tribes, and a race, dependent upon reproduction for survival.

Evolutionary psychology is particularly at odds with our embracing of sexual diversity. Having dismissed evolutionary psychology and any sense of heterosexual normalcy, we have no bounds to normality.

Losing our Sexuality

When human biology becomes uncertain, the fundamental dynamics between people become uncertain. Abnormal, unnatural desires might well be natural reactions to abnormal, unnatural circumstances and trauma. Losing our biology means losing our psychology. We are victims of our biological ambiguity, who do not notice we are victims.

Babies have no knowledge of sexuality, or very much else. Their sexual instincts unfold as they mature, in the company of others.

When gender becomes a social construct, then the link between gender and sexual desires becomes no less a social construct. Heterosexuality becomes a social construct because that individual born alone on an island cannot imagine heterosexuality any more than any other attraction.

The tribeless West having dispensed with biological gender, sexuality became lost in the mire. When gender becomes unreal, so do natural desires related to gender. Sexuality is caught up in our post-biological senses of what gender entails. We lose sense of our sexual instincts.

The result is unnatural gender and sexual diversity. In the conflicts between social mores and inclusion of all peoples around, we are inclusive. Inclusion matters more to us than people living lives in accordance with biological reality: males being male; females being female. It matters more to us than people living lives in accordance with their maturing natures: men desiring women and women desiring men, procreating, surviving.

Our eradication of gender and rejection of heterosexuality as the norm are never far apart. We think they are both human rights, but if we treated gender and families as biological facts, there would be less confusion giving way to feelings of being anything but heterosexual.

Gender Marxism

Gender ideologues insist that gender and heterosexual normality were Western inventions imposed by our male forebears to oppress a planet previously unaware of them. As it is with race, the ideologues are really rejecting the sciences the West once applied to everything.

Imagining that gender exists because men created gender is much like imagining that race exists because white people created race, and equally nonsensical. Races, genders, and everything else cannot create themselves.

Imagining that gender exists because white people created it is less intrinsically absurd, but no less absurd in fact. All the races on earth understood male and female, if only in the most obvious differences, by looking around at their tribespeople. They did not need white people to distinguish men from women, whatever words they used. Long before encountering white people, they felt the natural attraction between men and women and recognised its link to childbearing.

To believe that other races did not recognise race and gender until white people told them about race and gender is to believe that other races are completely stupid. Ironically, having become convinced that white people invented biological gender and heterosexual normalcy, gender ideologues accuse people believing in biological reality and sexual morality of white supremacy.

Ideologies can be best understood not as reason or intellect but as political assaults against the West. They often also reject other races, countries and cultures, but the ideologues are typically too fixated with their hostility to the West to notice that rejection, admit it, or care.

Gender ideology is gender Marxism. Normalising aberrant sexuality is sexual Marxism, in spite of the communists in office across Eastern Europe until 1989 and 1991 treating homosexuality as a crime against their societies and transgenderism then being unavailable. They had societies, of sorts.

Biological gender and heterosexuality are the foundations of families and so races, nations, and cultures. Rejecting one is rejecting another. Defending one is defending another. Moral degradation led, at least in part, to the fall of the Roman Empire.

The Europeans defying our new gender and sexual orthodoxy are not just religious and communal peoples like those of Poland but also countries like Russia and Hungary, edging back to being peoples again. Countries subjected to Soviet communism through the twentieth century resist returning to the tyranny of ideology.

Gender Identity

In its early years, feminism focused upon the interests of women in the context of race: identifying black men as particular threats to white women. When the West gave up our races, only the feminism remained.

Another division of the world we would not countenance by race or religion, gender became central to our post-racial identities. We do not like talking about race, but love talking about gender.

Freeing white women from white culpability after the Holocaust, white people's crimes became the crimes of an allegedly patriarchal West. Sensing white people to be the most dangerous creatures on earth, feminists became most worried about white men: the very group best able to protect white women, the only men who would. Western feminism became less interested in protecting white women from other races than in advancing all women at the expense of white men.

White feminists ceased worrying about men of other races. Worrying about them would be racist.

White men have become the same. Hostility to our gender separates white men from our gender, much as hostility to our race separates white people from our race. We might or might not protect women from other white men, but never from men of other races. That would be racist.

The tribeless West has had an increasing problem with maleness since the Second World War, but only white maleness. We chastise white men for sexism, real or imagined, but respect sexism among men of other races, however misogynistic and cruel. Anything else would be racist.

Sexism is like racism. Philosophical hoops ensure that only white people are guilty.

White people have become the least patriarchal people on earth, and might always have been, but that is not the point. To people consumed with hostility to white people, any vestiges of white masculinity is too much. Little wonder the West ran out of heroes.

Gender Nationalism

Our priorities being political and economic rather than social and refusing to recognise the interests of married couples being shared by those couples, the tribeless West considers men more powerful than women because men are more likely to reach political office or be rich. Having rejected families and society with our individualism, we do not recognise the paramount roles women once enjoyed in families and thus societies.

We no longer recognise gender typical behaviour, so can no longer imagine men more than women pursuing political power or money in the first place. Consumed by our new-found separation between the sexes, we cannot imagine husbands fairly representing their wives or male leaders fairly representing men and women, any more than we can imagine white people fairly representing people of other races.

Gender identities mean we treat men collectively and women collectively, rather than as individuals. We imagine a poor woman living in a trailer park being uninterested in her husband's job or income, but feeling inspired, or at least consoled, by a rich woman she does not know getting a little bit richer with another company directorship or reaching a little bit higher in her political career.

Such a poor woman is neither inspired nor consoled by rich women bettering themselves. Gender identities are for rich white women and Jewesses, competing with rich white men and Jews.

While the West denies race and culture, we are obsessed with gender. We accept, even presume, women will be loyal to their gender: a sort of gender tribalism or gender nationalism, although even gender cannot overcome politics in this Age of Ideology. We believe being of the same gender means women share affinity, but we do not imagine our affinity by race.

Women would not countenance such gender tribalism among men. Nor would men want it. White men are individuals. Men of other races have their races.

Our desire to protect white women from rape, violence, and other crimes once added to our racial discrimination. Our rejection of racial discrimination compromises our capacity to protect them.

We consider gender relevant to describing criminals as we no longer allow race or religion. If we are comfortable with public perceptions that men are more likely than women to commit crimes because those perceptions might save women's lives, we no longer allow the same for perceptions about race or religion. Thus we blame white men for the crimes of immigrant men and, in Europe's colonies, indigenous men.

We think it is perfectly reasonable to consider young men more unruly than elderly women, but completely irrational to consider young black men more unruly than elderly white women. If a thousand young black men were to come up and punch us in the mouth, we would think no worse of black people, black men, or young black men. We would baulk at being near young men in general. Refusing to be wary of someone by race, we would never look so easily at young white men again.

To protect women, we will segregate them from men, but not from other races. When there is a choice between advancing other races and protecting white women, we advance other races. Protecting white women would be racist.

The racial loyalties that mean nothing to white people remain all-important to everyone else. Coloured women side with the men of their race, as the men of their race side with them. White women imagine their affinity with coloured women while being enamoured with coloured men, but coloured women are hostile to white women they perceive as taking their men, by marriage or other relationship.

Gender identity does not help women. It does not help men. Gender identities divide us by gender more than sexism ever did.

There can hardly be a more destructive a division between people than that according to gender. The reality of procreation, as well as every instinct towards it, means men and women must get along, at least enough to reproduce.

Men and women need each other. Gender is our most unnatural of identities.

Sexism

We did not need science to distinguish male from female, although scientists once pursued understanding of what the differences between males and females entail. Like differences between races, we have increasingly fobbed away differences between genders since 1945 for fear they imply superiority of one over the other. We do not believe any traits are essentially masculine or feminine any more than we believe races have different traits.

Nature has not changed. Our instincts remain sexist.

Men are attracted by the colour red, possibly for evolutionary reasons. A rosy complexion in a female might indicate increased fertility.

Human instincts are also racist, which was our first reason to reject them. Only white people have rosy complexions.

The most reasonable explanations for many of the differences between men and women are biological, related to procreation. More often than not, when we complain about sexism, we are complaining not just about society but about evolutionary psychology intruding upon our ideology of individualism.

Men and women try to identify quality mates willing to commit to relationships by appearing self-confident, talking to others, and not being too accessible. Women use the tactics more than men, because the pregnancy risk requires women to choose males who will provide for them and remain with them.

Men choose women for their beauty. The curves that make women's bodies the most voluptuous facilitate childbearing.

Women choose men for security. It augurs well for parenthood.

A good husband is a good father. A man should marry a woman who will be a good mother.

Parents with both sons and daughters can hardly miss the differences in behaviour, development, emotion, and almost everything else between boys and girls. The hardest thing about raising girls is them expressing their emotions so much. The hardest thing about raising boys is them expressing theirs so little.

Girls hurt with words, boys hurt with fists. Boys' fights soon finish, girls' fights persist.

Those differences and their implications are no longer open to logical investigation, not in the West, even if we laughingly accept women cannot read maps and men are loath to ask for directions, without us trying to find women cartographers or men calling for help. Convinced as we are of equality, we blame differences around gender upon white men's sexism, whether conscious or not, much as we insist differences around race can only be due to white people's racism.

We speak of gender bias, but really mean gender. We think we can end gender if we end gender bias.

Gender and Language

In our fervent rejection of sexism, we have become fixated with what gender might mean. We are determined it mean nothing whatever.

As we did with race, we skewed language to further our ideological aims. All language is political anyway, premised upon people communicating with each other. That person born alone on an island has no language, perhaps not even in thought.

The feminine form of words faded from view, not simply to describe vocations we wanted women to take but also gendered pronouns. He and she became they, as if the singular became plural. Men and women became indistinguishable from each other and from a leather-covered settee.

Animals too lost their genders. Lions and lionesses all became lions. Sheep are still sheep.

Language conveys less meaning, as it is meant to do. The essence of our postmodern language is conveying as little information as possible. We think that makes language inclusive, but words without human traits strip us of humanness. They strip us of nature.

What was beautiful becomes bland. The only things blander than our language are the people we describe.

We give our children names equally one gender or another, so that not even they need know what gender they are. For boys and girls to be the same, they must all be neutered. Alternatively, one must become the other. If we are not feminising boys, we are masculinising girls.

People wedded to ideals over reality think and do all sorts of strange things in the name of equality. So do people hungry for attention.

Gender disappears. A child is androgynous, however absurd and confusing that might be and however much children might hate our grand ideological design.

Free Market Mental Health

Sigmund Freud, the inventor of psychiatry, understood the significance of evolutionary sexual desires, but complicated Western minds with Jewish ambiguities. Freud might have been rationalising his perversions.

Before Freud confused us, the Western way was simply to cut through with straightforward single-mindedness. If we feel fragile, then we are fragile. If we do not, then we are not.

Traditionally, mental illness was a physical illness of the brain, but our ideological West has little regard for anything physical, including brains. Mental illness was confusion, delusion, irrationality, or other unnatural actions or thoughts, but we have little regard for reality, reason, or human nature. Mental health became a political and social construct.

Our postmodern mental health may well be the archetypal postmodern medicine, for people demanding the right to think and feel whatever they want to think and feel. It is free market medicine, with customers dictating what constitutes good health. The most natural of feelings become mental health issues, if we dislike them. The most perverse of desires do not, if we enjoy them. (If wilful childlessness is an illness, then it is a terminal illness.) It is selectable sickness.

Mental illness offers us more identity options, since we refused our racial identities. For all our edicts of individualism, we narrow the ranges of statistically normal behaviour, categorising every increment of activity into long-winded syndromes and even longer-winded disorders. Labelling anything a disorder is a judgement, but syndromes avoid the judgement implicit in suggesting something is healthy or not.

We remove the notion of choice when liberty does not suit and our rights might convict us for the choices we make. So the list of mental illnesses further expands, trying desperately to be inclusive of all people. Mental illness becomes our excuse.

With the West becoming dysfunctional, Western families became dysfunctional. White people became dysfunctional.

We embrace all manner of psychological problems, but deciding people's behaviour is mental illness does not mean we cure them. That would be intolerant. We give them money, but only if they remain unwell.

Our fixation with economic growth is our growth in problems that people earn money redressing. Psychiatrists, psychologists, and other dedicated professional counsellors for hire give us options accordingly; our mental health issues are much too important to entrust to mere amateurs. Those professionals cure and lose customers who want to be cured, or that other people want to be cured, making for more customers to come.

Not everyone wants to be cured. Not everyone wants to be managed. Patients enjoying mental health services, and able to afford them if governments are not willing to buy them, do not want to be well. Counsellors are the affirming friends that patients pay to retain. Self-acceptance for purchase lasts no longer than the next therapy session.

From the viewpoint of mental health professionals, trying to change hapless lost souls who do not want to be changed would be unethical. It would be bad for business.

In matters of mental health, patients often prefer to adjust. We demand our rights to live with pain, longing, and trauma because we are coping, even if only just, instead of taking on the burden and risk of recovery.

When adjusting to our mental health problems is too difficult, we adjust our brains and rest of our bodies. It is good business for pharmaceutical companies.

Commercial pressures expand the realm of mental illness, thereby expanding the realm for treatments. Political pressures expand and contract those realms.

Mental Health for Dissidents

Much of what medical professionals label mental illnesses might simply be the fragility of individualism. It might be the stresses of diversity.

It might be people chasing endless liberties, suffering the tyranny of their desires. We have lost sight that loving people means setting rules and boundaries on their behaviour. Rules make adults and especially children feel safe and secure. So can the facts and norms of human biology.

The only oppression worse than too many liberties is too few. In our Age of Ideology, the most interesting mental disorders are those imposed upon dissidents, for beliefs and behaviours that powerful people are determined to change.

Communists reasoned their system was obviously perfect. Thus anyone not recognising that perfection must have been insane. For dissidents' own good, they were committed to mental institutions.

We have much the same approach, diagnosing dissidents with one phobia or another from a forever growing line of phobias from which those dissidents do not really suffer. A phobia can only be irrational, making each dissident the issue. The pesky recalcitrant must be mentally ill.

A diagnosis of a dissident phobia need not come from a medical professional. It can come from any person disagreeing with the dissident. When the lunatics think they are sane, all the sane people look like lunatics.

Without committing dissidents to mental institutions, the quaintly named sensitivity training is mental health treatment for dissidents in our ideological West. Powerful people want patients so sensitive to other people's feelings that they suppress their own, especially those feelings in the face of diversity however destructive or depraved. It is really insensitivity training.

There was a time we might have seen people acting strangely as evidence of their mental illness. We now regard spectators failing to celebrate that strangeness as suffering mental illness.

Whether a belief is true or feeling sincere does not excuse it, if that belief or feeling is insensitive to people whose sensitivities matter. For all our talk of equality, the sensitivities of some people matter more than the sensitivities of others, however depressed those others feel.

Our feelings are no longer natural. They are compliant. For all our talk of rights, we have lost the right to feel as we spontaneously would in the face of danger, depravity, or anything else threatening our tribe: our sense of society, civilisation, or anything else, even our life.

Transgenderism

Throughout Western history, the clothes we wore varied. At times, boys and girls in some countries wore dresses. Pink has been associated with boys at some times and girls in others.

There have also been people who have not followed the norms of their gender. A person pretending to be the other gender might have done so affectionately to entertain, or to sneak into a job she otherwise could not.

What did not change until the twentieth century was the very fact of being a boy or girl, man or woman. Amidst the breakdown of German society after the Great War, two German Jews founded the *Institut für Sexualwissenschaft* in 1919. Magnus Hirschfield, a homosexual, coined the German word for transsexualism in 1923.

Hirschfield pioneered the first instances of people thinking surgery could change their gender in the early 1930s. Those first few patients might have included at least one suffering the chromosomal abnormality Klinefelter syndrome, making him what we might now call intersex.

Something less than two percent of babies are born with biological glitches, leading a handful of children, teenagers, and adults to feel their genders are not what they appear to be or their sexual desires are not what they ought to be. Those glitches affirm the biological nature of gender and sexuality. Sometimes, nature goes awry.

They include hermaphrodites. They are not what we call transgender.

Capable of believing anything when reality does not constrain us, we began thinking a person could change gender soon after we began rejecting race, following World War II. Transsexualism entered the English language in 1949. People did not want to change gender before they were told they could.

At that time, we retained a sense that gender reflected a physical form. Changing gender required surgery.

In time, it would not. Gender change became easy.

Transgender Ideology

Dismissing the biological differences between people as political constructs from the past means we dismiss anything physical defining us. It also leaves us free to copy and create political constructs of our own.

Gender became postmodern because everything about the West became postmodern. Without race to define us, our postmodern rights to choose our identities and the reduction of gender to merely an identity mean we each have the right to choose our gender. We made gender an identity and stripped it of biology. Only the identity remains.

There is no gender reality because there is no biological or any other objective reality. There is only whatever gender and other reality a person perceives. It is gender by choice.

Like the rest of gender ideology, transgenderism is relativism. It is a rejection of fact in favour of each person's personal reality.

The so-called transgendered might not even be described as such. Unless they are declaring their transgenderism for whatever notoriety or political purpose they want, they are often described by their new gender as if they always were of that gender. Talk might be of their transgender experience, as others might talk of a past job or holiday.

Being ridiculous and divorced from genuine reality does not deter us. Gender became a matter of rights replacing reality, reality being so oppressive.

We are more interested in our rights to pretend than any rights to reality. We then equate the real with the pretend. That is our right.

Choosing our new genders and erasing our old, we allow people to change not only their current identification documents but also their birth certificates. We abandon not just the present but also the past to existential choice.

To describe people's biological gender as their gender randomly assigned at birth is to imagine doctors, midwives, and parents randomly pulling genders out of the air, instead of simply looking at them. In respect of each boy or girl, those assignors all reached the same conclusion.

Transgenderism is a social and political construct we are not willing to admit. There is no transgender for that person born alone on an island.

Our new social assignors are not assigning gender. They are assigning gender change.

Ideologues replaced the biological duality of life, male and female, with ideological dualities. Cisgender is anyone who is not transgender.

No longer male or female, we become male or female identified. Without biology to ground us, those identities are easily erased.

We abandoned biology with the delusion we are something else. People became political constructs.

Transgenderism and Sexism

Our reasons for ending discrimination against people wanting to change their gender are diametrically opposed to our reasons for ending gender discrimination. The gender we reject in other contexts, we respect if someone wants to change it. Gender is real, after all.

We dismiss the differences between genders when we reject sexism. We acknowledge there are differences between genders if people can change gender. They are just not biological.

Ours is gender without gender: without biology. Anything else would be sexist.

When the West rejected sexism, we rejected the idea of gender roles: that there is any gender-typical behaviour. Conversely, transgenderism is predicated upon there being gender-typical behaviour, albeit far more superficial than the behaviour we once recognised to be gender typical.

No longer thinking that gender determines behaviour, we think that behaviour determines gender. No longer are boys acting like girls or girls acting like boys. They become them.

The most trivial of gender-atypical behaviour, especially in children, is promptly diagnosed to be transgenderism. To define gender by gender-typical behaviour is to restore sexism.

A reason we rejected sexism is that women cannot choose their gender, which made sexism, like racism, unfair. (Life and the

universe are naturally unfair, but the ideological West chases
fairness.) Deciding people can change their gender should make
sexism fine. Being a woman cannot be too bad if some men choose
to become women and most women choose to remain women.
Transgenderism legitimises gender discrimination.

Everything feminists thought they had secured for women
became available to men calling themselves women. Every
protection women needed from dangerous men they surrendered
to men calling themselves women. Feminists resisting
transgenderism became radical feminists, although the only thing
radical about them was their engagement with biological reality.

To see the vitriol wielded upon women but not men resisting
so-called transgenderism reveals the deep misogyny in men
claiming to be women. The only people the transgendered hate
more than themselves are the gender they pretend to be.

Gender Validation

A Scotsman wearing a kilt does not become a woman any more
than a woman wearing slacks becomes a man. We have to *feel* our
gender.

Typically not claiming to be transgendered, transvestites often
wear the most garish of female clothes, hairstyles, and make-up,
accentuating female mannerisms. Like comedic impressionists, they
mock women more than they pretend to be women.

Perception is no longer at the periphery, for us born alone on
our islands. In the ideological West, gender depends upon
perception.

We prefer feelings to fact. Instead of relying upon biology, we
treat gender as being whatever someone feels. Giving credence to
feelings, gender becomes whatever he or she thinks it already is, or
is convinced by another person it already is.

Without biology to define us, our gender need not be what we
think and feel it is, if we later change our mind. A present of one
gender becomes a past of another. What we thought was our past
might not have been. Our new gender identity becomes our
supposedly true identity we have come to discover. Our past
gender identity becomes a false one, as we did not realise at the
time.

We can thus have two identities: one we realise was false, one we decide is real. They can be friends. It is an escape from reality: from the isolation of individualism.

For all our individualism, people insist that other people respect their stated genders. They demand that other people validate their genders, as if those genders are invalid otherwise.

The perceptions are not only ours. To be valid, whatever that really means, gender identities must also be everyone else's perceptions.

In ordinary conversation, people do not use pronouns to address each other, but there is nothing ordinary about our treatment of gender. Demanding that every spoken or written conversation validate a person's gender identity, we are supposed to begin every introduction by clumsily declaring our pronouns or by asking everyone else to declare theirs.

The only people declaring their pronouns, other than fawning politicians, seem to be people lying about them. Pronouns became pivotal to people's existence, for people without anything real in which to believe. They could stand at the gates of hell and expect Satan himself to ask them for their pronouns.

Satan probably will. God at the gates of heaven will not, but Satan at the gates of hell will.

Never is the narcissism of individualism more in evidence or more extreme than it has become with ideological gender. Having decided upon their gender and thus pronouns, the rest of the world is expected to kowtow to their lies and delusions, every moment and in every situation.

What remains of people without their supposed genders being validated by other people is not clear. Somewhere in the ether, there are presumably all the invalid people: unknown, unseen, not really existing, because the bigots do not bow down before them.

Among the many benefits of being engaged with biological and other reality is that we do not need strangers or anyone else to validate our genders. Biological gender does not require validation. Racial identities grounded in biology do not need validation. We are what we are, as everyone is.

SIMON LENNON

Gender Individualism

We can have different genders for different purposes. A lesbian can become a man, but her girlfriend remains a lesbian.

When gender becomes something we choose or we feel without facts corrupting us, it expresses our individualism. In our obsessive individualism we let people choose their realities, ratifying their feelings whatever they are, playing to their senses. We believe whatever pretence we can, whatever feels good: anything we think makes our lives better, whether it does or not.

With every apparent new freedom we find, we pursue the next: new extremes to living without rules or restrictions. Unconstrained by human biology, gender fluidity allows a person to change gender by the minute. We are all gender diverse.

Nor are our options for gender limited to the biological two. Without biology, we find no end of ambiguities to be.

The number of available genders grew, with each proponent trying to outdo the others. Any increment of thought or behaviour became a gender, if it was in any way referable to what we once knew to be masculine or feminine, and even if it was not.

Each gender is a fad. Fads soon pass. When the choice of gender is too much, being non-binary is a catch-all for being anything except male or female, or for being both male and female, or for being anything else.

Talk reached that of an infinite range of genders. We fulfilled another dream of perfect individualism.

With an infinite array of genders came an infinite array of names of genders. Some names people presumably devised for themselves.

Others names and definitions accompanying them, people seem to have devised for others, knowing that someone from a populace of solitary people chasing any identity they can find will choose it. Not that anyone will admit to choosing it. Instead, people will declare their great joy to have found the gender to describe them, as if they ever needed one. Everyone will be pleased.

An infinite array of genders implies an infinite array of sexualities to match. Every person on earth can have a unique gender and thus a unique sexuality, and then another, and another.

Sexuality is as fluid as gender. Gender individualism is sexual individualism. Feminism, homosexuality, and everything else become as obsolete as anything normal and natural has long become.

Gender Dysphoria

It is all very well to demand a right to choose our gender, but we do not always want rights. Few patients want personal responsibility for their mental well-being. Parents do not want blame for their children feeling miserable. Some people find believing that they or their children are in the wrong body to be less painful than believing they or their children are homosexual.

Conversely, a man who thinks he is a lesbian is a deluded heterosexual. A man saying he is a lesbian might simply be lying.

The same can be said of women thinking or saying they are homosexual men, although such women are much fewer than the aforementioned men. They do have the same incentives to lie.

Our identities are our choices to craft, up to a point. We have the right to nominate our gender without surgery, but will not resort to that right if we are trying to get a government or health insurer to pay for that surgery. Sometimes it suits us to imagine having no choice at all. We have reached the limits of our liberty.

What we call gender dysphoria is a person's feeling of being of one gender but born in the body of the other. For all our rejection of science, we like terms that sound scientific. Psychiatrists call it gender identity disorder because they think gender is a matter of identity. Either way, we are saying we have a gender inside us and a gender for our bodies. They might or might not coincide.

Ideologues created a sort of transgender biology. We treat gender as a social construct but not gender identity disorder, in the rules haphazardly put together. Gender suddenly is not just real. It is doubly real. Reality can be a problem.

We imagine gender to lie in something other than our bodies. What we are if we are not our bodies is not clear, but we are not trying to be clear. We are trying to accommodate people feeling whatever they feel, without judgement.

If it means we can have metaphysical souls of one gender and bodies of the other, then it is an amazing interpretation of what a soul might be. It is also a rare time we still believe in souls, or would believe, if we thought about what we believe. Nor do we wonder how anything could be bound to a physical body without being physical too.

If it means our brain can be of one gender and our body of the other gender, then it beggars belief how such a condition could arise. More significantly, we are acknowledging differences between male and female brains.

Again, our determination to accommodate people's desires to change gender falls afoul of our rejection of sexism. We are making gender biological, especially in our brains, with psychological differences between men and women.

Gender dysphoria is simply a sense that a person does not fit gender stereotypes. Anyone rejecting the idea of gender stereotypes should also reject the idea of gender dysphoria.

A person recognising gender stereotypes can still reject the absurdity of gender dysphoria. Some feelings are absurd.

Sex and Gender

Sex and gender used to be synonymous, before sexual acts became so talked about that talk of gender became more polite. Later, there came those who sought to escape the absurdity of transgenderism by distinguishing social gender from biological sex. That is to say, gender is a social construct because it is defined to be a social construct.

There is some basis for such a view. Men acting like women are not our traditional Western way, but they are traditional among a handful of other races. A scarcity of men can be a reason for some Polynesians to adopt female roles, for the good not of themselves but of their family or village. Biology remains.

There is no more deeply a feminine trait than being sexually attracted to men. Iran lets homosexual men live as women to escape the death penalty for homosexual acts. Other races and ethnicities speak euphemistically of a third gender to accommodate men not acting like men. They are generally social outcasts.

The ideological West does much more than that. Biology no longer remains. Without societies, there are no social outcasts.

When dissidents defending biological reality reject gender altogether, they effectively accept that redefinition of gender to be without biology. Biological sex remains.

Gender ideologues either dismiss biological sex to see only social gender, or they insist that sex and biology magically change when gender changes. Sex and biology become political and social constructs because they define them to be political and social constructs, with sex again synonymous with gender.

Many of the so-called transgendered admit they pursue something physical by bombarding their bodies with hormones and disfiguring their bodies with surgery, as a mere social role would not require. Believing that their body affirms their sense of their gender or not, gender ceases being a social construct to become again physical, if still not biological.

Gender affirmation does not require surgery. It requires an engagement with reality.

So-called gender affirmation surgery should properly be called gender falsification surgery. That some women's faces and body shapes appear so much like those of men and some men's faces and body shapes appear indistinguishable from those of women says less about gender than it says about surgery.

Surgery cannot create organs. It can only repair, reshape, mutilate, or remove them. Injections and surgery cannot transform people into people they are not.

A castrated man is not a woman. He is a eunuch.

Race and Gender

Once people disengage from reality, there is no logical limit. When people feel free to pick and choose one identity, they can pick and choose any identity.

To redefine being British, German, or anything else away from race to citizenship is the same as redefining man or woman away from sex to an ideological sense of gender. They both involve replacing human biology with political or social constructions. The mentality that thinks an immigrant becomes British because somebody or paperwork says so is the mentality that thinks a man becomes a woman because somebody or paperwork says so.

Recognising one biological reality means a person is more likely to recognise another. There are few more certain ways for a white person to be called racist then defining gender, families, or anything else by biology.

Rejecting gender flowed from our rejection of race, so believing in biological gender is akin to believing in race. They are intertwined.

The West having equated Nazism to racism, any white person recognising biological gender is also vulnerable to being called a Nazi, although the people who fought Nazis recognised the reality of biological gender no less than Nazis did. Everybody then did, outside the *Institut für Sexualwissenschaft*.

Conversely, where racial identity is confused, gender identity can also be confused. They are both human biology.

Biological definitions of people have none of the drama of ideological definitions. If race and gender are social constructs and our gender can change, then so can our race, although a white person claiming to be black reflects white privilege in our new racial hierarchy. Logically, a male claiming to be female should thus be accused of exploiting his male privilege.

The logic that lets a person choose his gender means he can choose his race, she can choose her species. Logically, gender self-determination should also allow racial self-determination and species self-determination.

As legitimate as gender fluidity would be racial fluidity. We can all be transgender. We can all be trans-racial. We can all be racially diverse.

The whole thing does not get any easier to fathom, but our piecemeal approach is not about fathoming anything. We are not trying to be logical. We are trying to be inclusive. We are finding reason to accept everyone whatever he or she feels (except anyone who disagrees), legitimising the illegitimate however absurd it might seem, so we can leave each other alone.

Rejecting Trans-Racism

Needless to say, the ideologues reject any similarity between white people pretending to be black and men believing they are women. They distinguish race from gender while calling both political and social constructs, but the distinctions are more political constructs.

They might see white people lying about being black while men sincerely believe they are women, but at least one woman claiming to be black felt she was black. Sincerity does not justify trans-racism as it justifies so-called transgenderism.

Amidst our politicised mental health, the ideologues respect gender dysphoria but reject racial dysphoria, but they also do not require a person to feel gender dysphoria to be so-called transgender. If choice is a reason to change gender it is not a reason to change race.

They are the contradictions when people begin with their conclusions, as ideologues do. They then work backwards looking for reasons they think support those conclusions.

Contempt for white people is never far away. Among the rationales for rejecting trans-racism is the presumption that race is grounded in violence but gender is not. It's the presumption that white people invented race to oppress other races, but in this case there is no presumption that we also invented gender to oppress women.

Meanwhile, the gender ideologues see gender-based violence all around them. It is all a matter of the moment and the conclusions they want.

Other rationales for rejecting trans-racism include the insistence that black people somehow suffer by white people pretending to be black, but that women do not suffer by men thinking they are women. It is more of the suffering by other races they do not need to feel for us to impute.

Meanwhile, women tell us they suffer from the violence that men commit in their spaces, especially women's prisons. Ideologues do not care about white women suffering. They turn away befuddled at the thought of women of colour suffering because of white men being treated as women.

Transgender Privilege

In much of the world, transvestism is entertainment, especially for men desiring women but not wanting to impregnate them. We are not the only people paying money to promote transvestism. We are the only ones paying it through government and for reasons other than our entertainment.

In our tribeless West, the so-called transgendered do not suffer discrimination. They enjoy privilege.

Far from punishing perversions, we reward them. For people pursuing another career, we encourage perversions.

Western democracies having become the rule of the minorities, sexual and gender minorities are the minorities white people can join. If white people want richer white people to notice them, and our governments to help them like we help other races, they had better be something other than heterosexual accepting their gender. It is much easier than getting a disability, and is the only empowerment some people feel.

Racial minorities are tribes. Sexual and gender minorities are not really tribes, but white people blind to the real tribes think they are.

The West loves victims: not real victims, but people denoted to be victims. Women are not minorities, but they enjoy victimhood status in the tribeless West as if they were.

Also denoted victims are homosexuals and the so-called transgendered, although not for their victimhood being self-inflicted. Without surrendering any of their financial privilege or lust for women, rich white heterosexual men can leap from the foot of the victimhood tree to the top simply by declaring themselves to be lesbians. In an instant, they progress from being the most maligned people on earth to being the most admired for their supposed bravery, but only in the immoral ideological West.

There is something particularly absurd about heterosexual men claiming victimhood status for being so-called trans-lesbians. Far from losing any privilege, they gain some.

Transgender Rights

So-called transgender rights are more than merely rights to dress or behave like people of the other gender. Everyone has that.

They are more than rights of a man to call himself a woman or a woman to call herself a man. Freedom of speech includes freedom to lie and freedom to express one's delusions.

They are rights to compel everyone else to say and to think what the so-called transgendered want everyone else to say and to think. They are rights to deny others their freedom of thought and of speech: their freedom to think the truth and to tell it. They are rights to impose their lies and delusions onto others: to force others to lie or to share their delusions.

Men calling themselves women demand rights unimaginable to normal men. They demand rights to enter women's washrooms that normal men do not want.

They demand rights to enter women's sports, winning medals and championships they could never win competing against other men. Normal men call that cheating.

Most notably, they demand sexual favours from lesbians. Women formerly free to rebuff men's advances can no longer rebuff them, without being called transphobic and even homophobic.

Those men have no desires for heterosexual men. They too are heterosexual men.

With women less likely than men to suffer aberrant feelings, it seems, far fewer women reject their biological gender. Those women calling themselves men are causing far fewer problems than the men calling themselves women cause.

Women do not need to call themselves men to play men's sports. If they are playing men's sports, they have no unfair advantage.

Women are not demanding the right to use men's washrooms or dressing rooms. If they wanted to join men there, many men would probably enjoy it.

Transgender Vulnerability

There is more freedom in facts to be what we are than in the confusion and pressures of thinking we choose something not ours to choose. Without ideologies redefining it, gender is simply a biological fact, without judgement. It need not be an identity. It is not a feeling.

When we make gender a feeling, we make ourselves vulnerable to our feelings. Decisions that are not ours to make become cluttered with feelings of matters untrue: feelings fostered in the absence of facts.

People deluding others are liars. People deluding themselves are tragedies. Around the ideological West, both are rife.

The confusion in our ideological West is not about behaviours. It is about biology.

No longer grounded in reality, gender becomes a particularly fragile identity. Where identity is fragile, people are fragile. Our gender-ambiguous West is a place of confusion and listlessness.

Biological gender does not squish anyone out. Defining gender without biology squishes everyone out.

In a West where everything is political or economic, so is gender. Changing gender is an industry; money is central to so much delusion. As with other industries, immoral suppliers pursue ever more profits. We need only follow the money.

Persuading people they are not the gender they obviously are, or that they can gain fame, fun, or anything else by supposedly changing gender, is cruel. When children are the victims, it is the cruellest of child abuse. Immoral adults feeling dissatisfied with their gender eagerly diagnose the same dissatisfaction in children to further their claim they were born that way, assisting their bids for legal recognition and for government and health insurance subsidies to pay for their treatments.

Falsehoods do not become true because people believe them. A substantial proportion of people thinking they are changing gender realise their gender was never the issue. They change gender back again, often realising they had never changed gender at all.

Whether we are supposed to trust them to know their gender when they changed gender or when they change back again is not clear. Not even gender fluidity comprehends people mistaking their gender.

Biological Self-Loathing

The so-called transgendered are not being who they are. They are pretending to be what they are not.

Gender became narcissistic because postmodernism is narcissistic, wholly dependent as it is upon each person's sense of reality. Biological and other objective reality do not matter. Other people do not matter.

There is something extraordinarily self-absorbed about a person thinking and feeling so much about his or her gender as to decide that it is not what biology dictates. Expending the time to try to change gender is effort for people with nothing else to do: no nations to build, no people to save, and no imagination to think of something useful to do. They are people with too much money or too much access to other people's money.

So-called transgenderism indulges people already indulged. Western parents have spent decades indulging their children, too lazy and too keen to be liked by their children (and indeed by anyone) to refuse their children anything. Wanting to be of another gender is just another demand by children and then adults without boundaries, not even the boundary of reality.

Those parents accede to whatever their little darlings demand. Parents unwilling to deny their children anything deny them reality.

Where celebrity is everything, transgenderism might be a game in pursuit of attention. It might be a lie or a delusion where facts and the truth are immaterial. It might be chasing identity for people without racial identities. It might be an attempt to escape misery or self-loathing.

Transgenderism might be an assault on people's society, families, or race. Nothing is more widely applauded than assaulting Western families and races.

People claiming to be transgender are not rejecting gender as a biological or other concept. They specifically reject their gender.

We dispense with notions of gender and race, except when there is a chance to hate ours. Rejecting our race and gender feels good to a people relentlessly rejecting white racism and sexism.

Gender suicide is suicide. Our self-loathing since two world wars and a holocaust is never closer to our core than in our biological self-loathing.

Homosexual Ideology

When heterosexuality was the only sexuality people contemplated, it did not need a name. Examination of homosexuality led to both words being coined in 1868 by way of contrast, although heterosexuality was not popularly described as such until homosexual activism arose in the 1960s, amidst a general revolt in the West against Western Civilisation, and civilisation generally.

Homosexuality was rare before the middle of the twentieth century. It was rarer still before the Great War. It was possibly entirely male.

Respecting our biological natures does not require a willingness to respect our parents and other preceding generations. It does require us not to dismiss everything about them out of hand.

Embracing homosexuality often reflects contempt for past generations. It can be quite nasty.

Homosexuality is a social and political construct. There can be no homosexuality (any more than heterosexuality) for that person born alone on an island. A person needs someone else of his or her gender to feel a homosexual interest.

We are again inconsistent. Heterosexuality and homosexuality make no sense without sexism, discriminating between the genders in which we direct our desires. Even bisexuality presumes genders, albeit without the sexism.

Only ideology could deem homosexuality to be the equal of heterosexuality. Nature does not.

Homosexuality unable to procreate remains plainly unequal to heterosexuality that might. Heterosexuality grows, homosexuality dies, but the tribeless West refuses any status to heterosexuality above homosexuality.

Biologically unequal, we deem the two ideologically equal. Without sense of families, tribes, and races, we treat what harms us as the equal of what helps us.

Political activists pressed the American Psychiatric Association to remove homosexuality from its list of mental illnesses in the 1974 edition of the *Diagnostic and Statistical Manual of Mental Disorders*. Much is made of the change, but only fifty-eight percent of psychiatrists ratified the change a year later. In its place was a category of sexual orientation disturbance.

That was replaced by ego-dystonic sexual orientation in 1980, as the Association kept coming up with more complicated scientific-sounding gobbledygook. Political pressures were not satisfied until it was removed in 1987.

We especially like equality among the unequal. It shows how much we have achieved.

In our postmodern politics of sexuality, it is not enough to end discrimination against homosexuals. In our ideological drive to equality, we demand heterosexual–homosexual equivalence without differentiation between sexualities, whatever the reality.

Marriage the West dismissed for being an institution when we only imagined it being heterosexual, we came to support for homosexuals. The smartest thing proponents of homosexual marriage ever did was call it marriage equality. We support anything connoting equality.

The tribeless West's acceptance of homosexuality is our further eradication of biological gender and the natural desires it entails but, paradoxically, there is nothing like our determination to promote homosexuality to restore talk about gender. Heterosexual spouses remain genderless partners, but not homosexuals marrying or registering civil unions. They are husbands and husbands, wives and wives.

Homosexual couples splitting into male and female roles suggest gender remains innate even in the face of homosexuality. For attention-seeking men, there is theatre in being effeminately homosexual. Butch lesbians are more frightening.

Other races connect marriage with parenthood. We no longer do. We do not connect parenthood to anything.

Homosexual Biology

A major reason for ceasing to treat homosexuality as a mental illness was that people chose it. Mental illness was reserved to desires and behaviours people felt were involuntary: a loss of personal control.

In much the same way, stealing is not a mental illness, although the compulsion of kleptomania is. People would not be mentally ill for being homosexual unless they felt compelled to it, imagining it to be natural to them. For homosexuals to decide they have no choice in being homosexual would be like thieves deciding they have no choice but to steal.

Believing we choose our gender should mean we choose our sexuality too, but we are trying to accommodate different foibles. The trouble with homosexuality being a choice was that morality came into play.

Morality legitimises discrimination. The best way to remove moral condemnation of homosexuality was to stop treating it as a choice.

We were not returning to the stigma of homosexuality being mental illness, so ideologues decided homosexuals were born that way. We cannot blame people for conditions to which they were supposedly born. Away from the realms of choice and morality, discrimination became untenable.

We ceased referring to homosexuality as a preference in favour of it being an orientation: innate, unchangeable. Believing that homosexuality is biologically determined ignores the reality of many homosexuals' preceding heterosexuality: before that painful divorce, for example. We thus tweak our language to make it seem like they were homosexual all along, but did not know it. They discovered it.

That people could be homosexual without realising it, even marrying someone of the other gender and bearing children, is preposterous. Being preposterous does not dissuade us.

In the tribeless West, we dismiss biological determinism, except where it suits us. We rejected unpalatable portions of human physiology around race and gender, but created a palatable new physiology around transgenderism and sexuality. Genders and heterosexuality are not biologically determined, we say, but gender identity and homosexuality are. Like transgender biology, ideologues invented homosexual biology as a matter of policy, not science.

We have gone from seeing people born to genders and choosing homosexuality to seeing people born to sexualities and choosing their genders: from seeing gender as biologically determined and homosexuality as a social construct the result of choice or environmental factors, to seeing gender as a social construct the result of choice or environmental factors and homosexuality as biologically determined. We have turned reality around.

Homosexual biology is not obvious. There is none of the physical or other observable features of race and gender. The only places these supposed homosexual orientations could hide are the places in which lie hidden the genders of people feeling gender dysphoria: if not their brains then some metaphysical selves or souls.

Male and female gave way to homosexual and heterosexual in a second ideological binary of life. When we think we are born heterosexual or homosexual instead of male or female, then a homosexual choosing to be a man is a homosexual man and one choosing to be a woman is a homosexual woman.

In practice, it is all more befuddled, but we do not think of the disarray. We look back at the end of it and believe the person saying then whether he or she was homosexual to start with. If the person changes his or her mind, we forget what he or she last said and look back again.

We have reached another limit of our liberty: finding sexual liberties our forebears never imagined; losing liberties our forebears took for granted. Where our forebears understood choice in homosexual activities, we dismiss it. Where our forebears examined environmental factors causing homosexuality, we flee any onus to wonder why homosexuals desire as they do.

It is a sort of homosexual eugenics. Talk occasionally turns to trying to identify a homosexual gene or something like it, while we dismiss the rest of eugenics. No homosexual gene has been found.

Evolutionary psychology suggests that only a person carrying genes so inherently awful they should not endure might be anything but heterosexual. If there were a genetic or other biological basis for homosexuality, then natural selection would soon cause it to become extinct because it prevents procreation.

Most likely, if there is a genetic or other biological basis for homosexuality then it is one leaving people vulnerable to the dysfunctional families and other environmental factors that foster homosexuality. Like gender dysphoria, it would be a biological basis for susceptibility to mental illness.

As with gender dysphoria, it suits adults wanting to think they were born homosexual, with all sincerity, to remember feelings from their past they never felt. They interpret natural childhood feelings as evidence of homosexuality that never were at the time. We are further away than ever from evolutionary psychology.

Animal Sexuality

A person determined to see aberrant sexuality in people or animals can always find it. The only evidence of that sexual aberration might well be our belief it is there, but in this Age of Ideology, belief suffices.

Applying our ideologies of inclusion and equality to animals garrottes the study of animal biology, much as we have garrotted the study of human biology. What we have not killed, we corrupted.

We interpret the rare incidences of apparently homosexual actions in animals as evidence of homosexuality being natural, without possibly knowing the thoughts inside animal heads. There is little or no evidence of animals feeling romantic love of any kind.

Physical stimulation is no more evidence of attraction in animals than it is in people. That stimulation might simply be with whatever is nearby.

Given the opportunity, a woman can arouse any man, however homosexual he might insist he is. If that arousal is purely physical, then so is homosexuality.

Apparent homosexual activity between animals, especially males, might express dominance and power by one animal over another. Homosexual activity between people, especially men, might be the same.

Conversely, without words to speak or hands to shake, incidences of apparent homosexual acts between animals might be forms of greeting or bonding. They might no more sexual in nature than Frenchmen greeting each other with kisses on their cheeks.

Socialisation

The most publicised claims of animals engaging in apparently homosexual acts or lifestyles relate to animals in zoos. The best of zoos remain unnatural environments, with small populations limiting the socialisation that animals, like humans, need. All sorts of odd things happen in captivity.

Animals in their natural environments among their natural populations engage in procreative behaviours. They have opportunities to do so.

In the wild, animals do not mate across species as we promote mating across races. Mules are not born in the wild, and might be better understood as the products of sexual assault rather than mating. Mules are normally sterile.

If we animalised humans instead of humanising animals, we would again see gender, race, and species as real. We would again see tribalism, heterosexuality, and childbearing as normal: our instincts to survive and procreate. We would impute the evidence of maternal devotion in animals to people. We would welcome patriarchy and matriarchy.

We would see the benefit of socialisation. Teenage male hormones target the best that is nearby, so that boys are more likely to experience homosexual desires in unnaturally masculine environments, especially where homosexuals recruit.

There might sometimes have been a fashion for a few boys and young men without female influences around them to pleasure themselves with other boys, or to have no sexual lives at all, during their single-sex school, university, and military days. Almost all of them left the fashion when offered time with women, marrying women when they could, with the support of the men with whom they had been intimate.

If we think aberrant behaviour by some animals means homosexuality is natural, we should think the same of necrophilia. Both occur among animals without socialisation.

It is the same for humans. Society would deter that person born alone on an island from carnal relations with a shell.

Homosexual Revisionism

The most determined of ideologues now interpret gods of ancient religions, even Jesus Christ, as being homosexual. Those claims would have shocked ancient adherents to those religions and Christ Himself, if anything could shock Christ.

Classical Greek men are often cited in support of homosexuality, but the essence of Platonic love was that it was not physical. Greek men married women and bore children.

The rare instances of homosexuality among our forebears could have been a problem for the claim that homosexuals are born homosexual. If homosexuality were biologically determined then there should have been at least the same proportion of homosexuals among our forebears as there are today. If anything, their proportion should have been greater in the past for their genes being less likely to be passed onto the next generation.

Instead, incidences of homosexuality have risen rapidly in recent years. Our great sense of enlightenment and enthusiasm for homosexuality keeps us from seeing that increased incidence as symptomatic of something having become wrong with the West.

Without any evidence to support them, ideologues insist that the past was rife with homosexuals trapped in heterosexual lives, even if those fools were unaware of it. We have more reason to accuse our forebears of oppression, as the tribeless West likes to do.

Homosexuals are not so trapped in modern films, television programmes, and books portraying the past. They are public and relaxed about their homosexuality, as is everyone else.

Those portrayals are completely untrue. The cultural and historical revisionism by which films, television programmes, and books promote multiculturalism also promote homosexuality, depicting both as norms throughout Western history they were not.

There is no end of fictional Western television and film characters either proud of their homosexuality or for whom it is incidental. Heterosexual characters so well adjusted to the world would be boring, marks of poor writing.

Conversely, television programmes portraying loving parents and happy children (at least white ones) have become fewer. Their thoughts are of love and loneliness, not children and childlessness. Parents break apart, or fight as if they should.

Promoting Homosexuality

A growing proportion of a lifestyle that natural selection would tend to diminish can only be a product of choice or environmental factors: another political or social construction. At least since the 1980s, there have been great efforts to promote homosexuality in the West.

Influential people changed the language, as influential people often do. Being gay had been another euphemism for homosexuality since the 1960s, when homosexuality was still a criminal offence, but was too commonplace a word not to appropriate altogether. Marketing homosexuality, gayness implies something merrily carefree, as nihilism can be.

Gay is also a gentle word. Homosexuality sounds much cruder, especially around children. Much less confronting than lesbians, gay women can sound appealing.

Paternalistic rules of language much like those we apply to race, we apply to sexuality. Abbreviating homosexual to "homo" is offensive. Abbreviating heterosexual to "hetero" is not.

We are just as delicate with people claiming to be transgender. Nobody objected to transistor radios being called "trannies," as they object to the so-called transgendered being described as such.

If we think people are born heterosexual or homosexual, there is nothing to promote except tolerance. The compliant West became tolerant of homosexuality, but the promotions continue. Promoting tolerance of homosexuality is promoting homosexuality.

If we have money for anything, it is for promoting homosexuality: our Straight Person's Burden. When we are not denying our heterosexual instincts, we are trying to kill them in others.

News services report romantic tales of homosexual relationships for no other reason than their being homosexual, without talk of domestic problems. Reports overcoming heterosexual stereotypes are really overcoming heterosexuality.

We consider a person's homosexuality or so-called transgenderism relevant to them being victims of crime and prejudice. We deem those descriptors irrelevant to them being perpetrators.

The tribeless West does not just promote homosexuality. It bans us from promoting heterosexuality.

Inclusiveness is selective. Offence is also selective. Promoting heterosexuality offends. Promoting homosexuality does not.

In the tribeless West, debating the idea people are born homosexual is intolerance. Suppressing debate about it is not. We can call homosexuality natural, but not heterosexuality.

We think we have found sexual freedoms, but they have become other people's freedoms to dissuade us from discovering our innate human instincts. Among the slavish followers of fashions and fads and among simply the psychologically vulnerable, people who might have never otherwise imagined homosexuality succumb.

Sexual Identity

No longer do we talk of people merely feeling homosexual desires or performing homosexual acts. They are homosexuals. Sexuality other than heterosexuality is another form of identity for people without racial identities, or without racial identities they want. Women are lesbians whenever they also want a gender identity, distinct from homosexual men.

In the tribeless West, gender has become the identity we choose. Sexuality has become the identity we do not. Race and ethnicity are something else entirely.

Homosexuality has become for white people everything that race remains for everyone else. We have become enraptured with homosexuals because we have become enraptured with minorities, equality, and inclusion.

Like other identities, homosexual identity demands equality, until it achieves equality. It then demands more. Homosexuality has become something to talk about, even boast about.

As we do with other races, we believe sexual minorities telling us they suffer due to prejudice, although their supposed suffering in the West is hard to find. Human rights are for homosexuals, not heterosexuals (among white people).

We can be so completely immersed in our gender identities we shut ourselves off from the other gender, encouraging the other gender to stay away. Homosexuality expresses the conflict between genders increasingly rife since we lost racial unity, but our tolerances leave us oblivious to the misandry intrinsic to lesbianism and misogyny intrinsic to male homosexuality.

If homosexual men do not hate women, they objectify them. Their fashions deny women their femininity; wanting models to be thin means wanting women too thin for bearing children. They style women's hair distinct from women's minds beneath their bland soft scalps.

Heterosexuals are not all free of misogyny or misandry, but we ignore the misogyny in homosexuals that we condemn in heterosexuals. We ignore misandry in anyone. If feminist lesbians understood how much misogynistic men enjoyed lesbianism, they might cease being lesbians.

If we retained our racial identities, we would not need sexual identities. They have not ended with homosexuality.

When homosexuality became pedestrian in the West, so-called transgenderism became the revolutionary fad. With homosexuality and transgenderism main stream, queerness became the rejection of family, race, and civilisation. Queer is anything abnormal: a catch-all for anything but heterosexuality comfortable in biology.

Without human biology, a mishmash of supposed genders and sexual orientations arises. They excuse people from personal responsibility for their or their children's perversions.

Asexuality lacks desires for anyone. It is individualism without even pretending to be anything else.

Like genders, ideologues also invent sexual desires, like Ray Blanchard's creation autogynephilia in the 1980s. No longer examining perversions, people create them.

Our ambiguities around sexuality and gender meld into a single ambiguity when the West adopted yet another gender option: genderqueer. It is sexuality as gender, with both whatever a person wants them to be.

Without racial identities, perversions offer a near-endless array of identities from which the lonely seekers of identity can adopt one or more as their own, from the widening choice available. They thus offer people tribes. As each perversion becomes pedestrian, a still more perverse lifestyle becomes the leading-edge identity and attention getter: the avant-garde weapon against normality.

Homosexual Nationalism

Linking homosexual men to lesbians is a political device. They often keep apart from each other.

We rejected racism and sexism for separating people, but our post-racial identities are no less a separation than race. Away from that island, homosexual identity depends upon public perception as heterosexuality does not. Homosexuals have their own radio stations, newspapers, bars, parties, and flag.

That there is a homosexual flag is most telling. Heterosexuality does not come with a flag. Determined to make the worst of all worlds appear the most beautiful, sexual minorities and the so-called transgendered adopted a striped rainbow as their flag.

They are the rainbow people, much like the multiracial children we also associate with rainbows and everyone else claiming minority status in a West enamoured with racial, gender, and sexual diversity. It does seem multiracial children are more likely than others to become homosexual, presumably in a more desperate pursuit of some kind of identity.

Rainbow people are our model individuals, but rainbows are not real. They are simply perception. Everything is perception, in the ideological West.

With identity comes tribalism. With homosexual identity came homosexual nationalism. Homosexual white people with no thought of loyalty to someone by reason of their shared race or country will rush to aid someone for no other reason than being homosexual.

When homosexual white people talk of their people, they mean other homosexuals. When homosexuals of other races speak of their people, they mean their race.

Sexual Contraception

Some people clearly choose homosexual behaviour. Denied conjugal rights with their spouses, prisoners in gaols might engage in homosexuality in prison but not outside it. Sexual activities are not their identity.

Others appear to feel compelled to homosexual desires. That does not mean those desires are natural. It means we are in the realms of wondering what caused those feelings of compulsion.

Before we stopped investigating environmental explanations for homosexual behaviour, evidence suggested that increased population density increased incidents of homosexuality. Homosexuality reflects pressure not to procreate, which might have contributed to Asian countries becoming crowded also becoming tolerant of homosexuality, at least officially.

Without racial identities and suffering the effects of immigration, we of the West feel pressure on the planet's population that other races do not. Homosexuality is birth control.

Homosexuals denigrating heterosexual men and women for being breeders, even when those heterosexual men and women are not parents, express the hatred of children that homosexuality can be. Hostility to heterosexuality is hostility to families and children.

One might cause the other, or something else might cause both. Correlation need not be causation.

Homosexuality is sexuality without the chance of anyone falling pregnant. When young female university and college students are lesbians until graduation in order to avoid falling pregnant (and other commitment), that is contraception. It is hard to imagine a greater disservice to the rest of their lives than thinking they are anything but heterosexual.

Whatever his or her motivation, any fertile person's sexual activity incapable of producing children is contraception, although it does not matter too much when it is temporary. Homosexuality is sexual suicide when practiced forever to the exclusion of childbearing.

It is not just homosexuality. Contraception remains close to every rejection of human heterosexuality. Contraception is no less contraception when homosexuals adopt.

Homosexual Adoption

Traditional adoption made the interests of children paramount. Only step-parents, financially and otherwise secure married couples, and the like could adopt.

Among the basket of rights we treasure in our tribeless West, some people's rights prevail over others. However much some people couch their cases in the language of children, the rights of adults matter more than the interests of children. Adoptive parents no longer need to be heterosexual.

Like gender, Western parenthood has become identifying as a parent. Without regard for biological relationship, a child may have three parents.

What nature does not envisage, commerce provides. Without motherly biology to bear or feed a child, a woman can offer for hire.

The more we pursue pretend liberties, the less we enjoy liberties to be real. We have more things to ban. We ceased referring to mothers and fathers as mothers and fathers, accommodating people who are not.

We pretend people who are parents are not. We pretend people who are not parents are.

Promoting homosexuality means we neuter motherhood and fatherhood into parenthood, but we reinforce gender for homosexual couples raising children. Men and women are parents when children have mothers and fathers, but when both self-identified parents are women they become mums. They are dads when there are no mums at all. Mothers' and Fathers' Days so exclusionary when children have only one available parent become all the rage when children have two supposed mothers or two supposed fathers.

The proportion of homosexual women mothering children is small and the proportion of homosexual men fathering children even smaller, but there is nothing like homosexuality to bring positive mention of raising children into our children's classrooms. Western concerns about population growth vanish to welcome homosexual parenting. Homosexual child-raising becomes another tribeless Western norm.

Much as it is with single parenting and traditional adoption, homosexuals raising children are not able to provide children relationship with at least one of their parents. Parents of both genders offer children learning and even mentorship upon which those children might wish to model themselves. They provide a child's origins.

Alternative tutors and mentors, such as grandparents, offer much, but their inspiration and impact depend upon them being allowed time with the children to teach them. Among the many factors in a child's environment are his or her guardians' attitudes to sexuality and gender.

Some guardians inadvertently promote homosexuality to their charges. Some homosexuals are more wilful.

Children have better mental health if raised by their parents, although adults determined to promote homosexuality deny it. In spite of our ideological decrees otherwise, parenthood remains in reality biological.

In the tribeless West, a child's well-being is immaterial. So is an adult's.

Homosexual Despair

There used to be considerable psychological and other analysis about the persistent pains, unfulfilled needs, and experiences that lead to homosexual feelings in small numbers of people, mainly men. Much as we dismiss old scientific data about race, we dismiss those analyses for defying our insistence that homosexuals are born homosexual. Intellectually credible those analyses and resultant hypotheses might be, they became ideologically unacceptable.

Unnatural desires are drawn not from biological natures but from unnatural environments. Why some people respond to their situation with homosexuality and other people do not is the same question we could ask about any environmental influences upon people's feelings and behaviours.

If we have choice, then we choose in the context of our environment and experience. People are more likely to become homosexual if they are told homosexuality is acceptable, even normal. No experiences drive people to homosexuality if they know us all to be heterosexual, if they have never contemplated anything but heterosexuality.

To defend efforts promoting homosexuality on the basis of the high rates of suicide attempts by homosexuals is to ignore the likelihood that suicide attempts are due to the same factors leading those people to homosexual desires. Counselling those people depends upon identifying those factors. Caring for homosexuals means recognising that homosexual desires might be symptomatic of mental health problems.

If people who believe they are ugly are disproportionately more likely to be homosexual, then it reeks of poor self-esteem about their physical appearances, however clever they might be and whatever they might achieve. It could be a form of evolutionary psychology.

Some people are so desperate for physical intimacy, even love, they accept whatever is available. Bad relationships are common precursors to people becoming homosexual, particularly abusive relationships or those ending with the other party's infidelity.

Women pained by abuse from men through their childhoods might feel love is better with other women, who will not abuse them. Dealing with their betrayal by those men, recovering their lives and letting go of their pains, at least in part, can mean they are no longer lesbians.

Homosexuality is soulless, a lifestyle for empty people. Denying people a chance to heal from the hurt in their hearts is extraordinarily cruel, but that is what we do when we tell them their homosexuality is innate.

Failed Parents

Sigmund Freud believed homosexual desires reflected people's desires to reconcile with their parents or other people important to them of their gender, craving for those people to love and remain with them. Their natural longings were not for people in general of their gender but for specific parents, spouses, or others.

The increased incidence of homosexual behaviour among later-born sons than first-born sons is not evidence of a biological component to homosexual behaviour, because a person's order of birth in a family is an environmental matter, without any biological component. Any younger sons' homosexual desires could well reflect them feeling less loved by their fathers more distant from them than from their older brothers.

Young homosexual men do not talk of their parents or family, suggesting that individualism and the breakdown of families in the West has contributed to increased homosexuality. Some children, especially only children, never recover from the trauma of their parents separating and divorcing when they were young. They might become homosexual to avoid the risk of their marriage traumatically ending.

Homosexuals do not want to be like their parents, at least in some respect important to them. They typically do not want to be parents at all.

The drive for homosexual marriage was always a drive for equality more than a drive for marriage. Homosexuality is a rejection of family.

Absent fathers appear to be primary causes of male homosexuality. Those fathers might remain married but work so hard or remain so emotionally or physically distant as to be absent.

If those in their abandonment are not craving their absent parents, they are loathing them. They might be both.

Those men missing their fathers might also blame their mothers for their fathers not being there, particularly if those mothers are there to blame. Homosexuality is their misogyny.

Fathers abandoning their wives and children might also cause female homosexuality in their wives and daughters. Homosexuality is their misandry.

Perhaps more commonly, absent fathers might contribute to their daughters becoming promiscuous with men. The same dysfunctional forces leading to homosexuality in sons can lead to promiscuity in daughters. Women are much less likely than men to become homosexual.

Fatherless young coloured men can join gangs, but gangs are normally based upon race and white people no longer have race. Anyone can become transgendered or homosexual. Some people become both, but since nobody is truly transgendered, those people are not truly homosexual either.

The last thing we in the tribeless West want is any suggestion we should not do whatever we wish to do. We demand the right to neglect and even abandon our spouses and children at will; it is our lives, not theirs.

Preferring to believe we are not responsible for others, it does not suit us to think our neglect or abandonment of our families could have a role in fostering homosexuality in our children. We think only that parents of other races have roles in fostering gangs.

Tolerance

Morality is hard. When it needs to be, love is forthright, strong, and tough. Thus so is morality.

Tolerance is easy. It is lazy.

There have always been people with personal problems, but we are no longer societies to help them. Trying to be tolerant, the rest of us individuals accept whatever thoughts and behaviours in other people do not obviously harm us, as individuals. Gender ideology depends on it.

There are no societies of tolerance. There are only individuals practicing personal tolerance and demanding tolerance from others. Relieved to be responsible to no one, no one is responsible to us.

Tolerance is not a foundation for a civilisation. It is an impetus for isolation, neglect, and decay.

In our rush to leave people alone (except the dissidents who care about them), we are excused from examining people, even when they ask to be examined. Troubling sick people with facts that might cure them becomes like a doctor telling patients they are seriously ill, depressing them. We are to let sick people stagger through their truncated lives to their premature deaths, instead of telling them the means by which they can be well.

We do it with people. We do it with the West.

Caring about each other has become unacceptable intrusion, if caring means disagreeing with something a sick person says. Disagreement is insensitive, to people so meekly compliant.

Leaving people alone is not compassion. It is indifference.

When we accept, we abandon, refusing to judge or even opine. In the spirit we call tolerance, nobody cares.

Our acceptance is our disinterest. Whether people really feel fine or not, feel proud or not, we leave them to their grave self-destruction. "Live and let live," equates to "Live and let die."

Hell, in the name of diversity, we like people's predilections and perversions. They amuse us. If not indifference, there is applause, from us spectators of other people's shows. They are oddities in the circus to watch.

The Age of Immorality

Diversity depends upon tolerance. Diversity depends upon immorality.

Our forebears feared we would lose our Western mores to the worst of other races' sexual plays and decadence if we let them close. Even so, like much of our history, our downward trajectory since the two world wars is far more obvious with hindsight than it would have been to predict beforehand.

Having lost the stomach to enforce our mores after World War II, the wartime generation relaxed laws prohibiting adultery in Britain. The West has progressively given up moral codes because we thought they were ours, but they were never only ours.

The first post-war generation wanted love without limits or inhibitions, but only imagined love to be heterosexual. Without societies or families but being simply individuals, the following generation's rebellion against preceding generations embraced homosexuality, chasing life without limits.

We used to be concerned about homosexuals for being estranged from society and so lacking social mores and empathies. We are no longer concerned. Since we became individuals, heterosexuals have little trace of social mores and empathies either. Within a generation, we went from seeing homosexuals as the furthest fringes of society to having no sense of society.

Rejecting heterosexuality as our biological norm was a rejection of our biological instincts, but we have no more reason to end our sexual free markets with homosexuality than our rejection of physical and psychological differences between people ended with race. With homosexuality having become socially acceptable in the West on the basis that homosexuals are supposedly born that way, others are also claiming they were born with their aberrant desires: what they call love. Deeming one desire equal to another, there is no reason to stop.

Debaucheries hidden in homes and bordellos moved onto the streets, competing for attention in a tribeless West where attention is everything and morality archaic. Not content with acceptance, their public parading defies families from which they came. They are defying any sense of society and civilisation, declaring their individualism: their separation from others.

Some men, perhaps women, dress as babies, to be treated as such. Their only clothes are nappies.

Others dress as dogs, to be lead around from leather leads. Leather masks seal their mouths.

Sexual liberty becomes sexual anarchy. Finding new liberties to demand, new depravities to demonstrate, is becoming harder and harder.

Having ceased being discriminatory, dolls can be partners. Technosexuals are attracted to robots.

We do not think any desires are natural, as much as we think they all are. Thus none can be unnatural. There are no perversions, because there are no norms.

One woman married a truck. Another married a poplar tree.

Claiming all love is equal makes none of it meaningful. Equality makes most things meaningless.

We dispensed with biological differentiation between people on spurious moral grounds after the Holocaust. We have ended up without morality at all.

Paedophilia, zoophilia, and necrophilia remain socially unacceptable paraphilia on the basis that other parties cannot consent. If powerful people decide no one is hurt and no harm is done, consent becomes immaterial.

Perhaps people can consent to necrophilia before they die, presumably setting it out in their wills. Many countries impute people's consent to organ transplants after their death. We might yet impute dead people's silence as their consent to necrophilia.

We are bigots whenever we fail to keep up with the perversions that powerful people decide are not perversions at all. Ours is the Age of Immorality.

It is hard to think of any issue plainer than sexuality on which the unnatural, tribeless West should step back and see the craziness of what we are doing. If the West retained any sense of morality, normality, or nature, we would take stock of the worsening depravity and debauchery on display at many a public festival of supposed sexual pride. Instead of treating it all as something separate from us watching from the sidelines, we would immediately recognise our dire need to correct our collective selves.

That would be nationalism or other tribalism. We should have done so decades ago. We have become freaks in other races' eyes.

Communities without Community

It is easy to see a half-century trail through the dissipation of our biological identities into the end of our communities. Without families and sometimes with them, white people find the world increasingly lonely. Crowds keep us from knowing anyone and anyone knowing us. Our inclusiveness leaves us alone. Nothing divides us. Nothing unites us.

Nobody hates. Nobody loves. Nobody cares.

Individualism is intrinsically incompatible with any sense of community. We cannot talk of being a society when the rights and entitlements by which we are possessed are not those of us all together but those of each of us alone. Society depends upon a greater purpose or common good, to which people freely defer. Society depends upon tribalism.

Our families do not stay together and our friends do not hang around anymore, but we have come to see families and other communities not as our strength and support but as constraints upon us doing whatever we want to do. Unwilling to abide impositions upon each individual us, we bask in the freedom we perceive solitary people to have. We do not need to have been born alone on an island to want to live alone there: unfettered by anyone else.

Losing our communities cost us more liberties than we gained, and not simply for being afraid of stepping outside. We have no laws of morality but an abundance of other new laws restricting us. We reduce our interaction with everyone.

With the end of single societies and our real communities, there arose what we call the communities. For all our individualism, there is hardly a concept we allude towards more often than community: hardly a delineation of people we do not call a community, however little its members interact with each other.

When we think of a group of which we are part, it is not race, country, or religion. It is rarely family. It is sport, creative arts, clubs, school, friends, and the like, although none of those groups reach very far or mean very much.

When we tire of one, we join another. It is superficial and transient, as chosen groups must be, but we do not mind. They are the communities individuals want: the company of strangers.

Our only societies were ever our people. With identity comes community. Our uniquely Western quest for a post-racial identity is the quest for a post-racial community.

Without society, our family is our best community. The only word we freely use and misuse more than community is family. Most groups of people, even nations, we call communities we also call families. We confuse metaphor with reality.

The last communities amidst our diversity are all minority groups. If they were not minorities, they would not be communities. Amidst Western multiculturalism, we are not the only races feeling lost.

Sexual Individualism

Might the same despair or other factors that lead people to embrace homosexuality, if not engage in it, lead them to embrace multiculturalism? Might the disinterest in sustaining a family that tolerates sexual diversity be as much a disinterest in sustaining a race and culture that underpins racial and cultural diversity?

Conversely, might those of us who treasure our childhoods, want to restore them for our children? Caring for our compatriots, might we want the same for them too: children, families, and communities? That is morality.

If we were still comfortable with our racial identities, our lives would still be grounded in biological reality. We would still enjoy our families and communities of people caring for each other. Not so many of us would think of being anything but heterosexual.

Heterosexuality is the sexuality of the connected: the tribe and family, even if individuals rarely feel it. Homosexuality and other aberrant sexualities are the sexualities of the disconnected, as much from the tribe and family as one's natural self: sexuality for individuals. Biological individualism gives way to sexual individualism.

The more isolated we are, the more we need a tribe. Heterosexuality can hardly be the basis for feeling part of a community when almost everyone, if not everyone, is heterosexual anyway. Every other sexual desire founds a make-believe community in our tribeless West.

So do all of them together, described by an interminably lengthening array of letters abbreviating words upon which not even their proponents agree. When keeping up with the letters became too difficult, people simply added at the end the mathematical symbol for addition: plus.

All a person requires for membership of this mythical community is being something other than heterosexual believing his or her biological gender. We can pick a perversion.

It is not real. When men pretending to be women threaten lesbian spaces, the community such as it is fractures: retaining some abbreviating letters, expunging others.

Homosexual acts are not akin to heterosexual acts. Homosexuality is narcissistic sexuality; no heterosexual couple looks so much alike as do some homosexual couples.

Our sexual individualism becomes absolute. No person is more completely self-absorbed than the woman who married herself.

At its core, homosexuality remains sexual individualism, even in a crowd. Without female influence insisting upon familial stability and other social mores, male homosexuality is an especially solitary sexuality. It is a sexual practice of self-contained people, with anonymous trysts and promiscuity about which heterosexual men only dream and which few heterosexual women want.

Marriage ceremonies do not seem to diminish homosexual promiscuity. No more a community than the rest of us individuals, homosexuals remain free to exploit and abuse each other. They might even enjoy it.

Heterosexual adultery seems rarer than homosexual adultery. It is certainly less brazen: a secret, a lie, between people knowing it is wrong. Heterosexual spouses consider adultery wrong, while homosexuals often do not care.

Respect

Respect that people once earned, they have come to demand. Like the rest of their rights, they demand to receive what they are unwilling to give.

Sad as it is, homosexuals do not respect themselves, however narcissistic they might be. It is hard to like people who do not like themselves.

Nor do people pretending to be another gender to that biologically determined or pretending to be no gender at all. If someone does not know another person's pronoun upon meeting him or her, then something is wrong with at least one of them.

White people delude ourselves into thinking a superficial self-centredness is self-love, so profoundly remiss, not just among homosexuals and the so-called transgendered. It is not self-love but self-delusion. With real self-love, collectively or individually, people procreate. Not loving themselves means people are not very good at loving anyone else.

Rarely is our indifference to others more obvious or convulsion with self-hatred more visible than it can be among homosexuals and other sexual minorities. Never does the human need to feel part of a tribe seem more determined and desperate, chasing some kind of a chance of community with all that entails: an instant of being noticed, if only with contempt.

We are not supposed to help people. We are supposed to respect them, but the greatest respect we can give people is to tell them the truth, whatever they happen to think. The kindest way to treat people is to ground them in biological reality and normalcy.

Were we to value facts and knowledge of facts, we would know there is no greater right than the right to tell the truth. No right is more useful or necessary to a person or people surviving and prospering than the right to tell the truth and thus the right to hear the truth from others.

Unwilling to acknowledge objective reality, alone aboard our metaphorical islands, the postmodern West has become consumed with fantasies each one more fanciful than the last. Being individuals, we lack the tribespeople with stakes in our lives to care, much as we have no tribespeople about whom we care.

No person is born alone on an island. What societies make of biology is premised upon biology nevertheless. Insisting human biology is immaterial does not make it disappear.

Our greatest liberties lie in lives freed to be our natural, biological selves: men desiring women or women desiring men, procreating, surviving. *Vive la différence!*

Enforcing Diversity

In a free society, people ought to be free to laugh at men pretending to be women. People ought to be free to laugh.

Humans seem to have an innate hostility to homosexuals and contempt for transvestites. It is sometimes manifest in violence, especially by other homosexuals.

Sexual diversity and transgenderism do not come naturally. We need to force them.

No other race tolerates homosexuality as the Jews and we now do, but we do not think in such terms. Like other intolerances, when we encounter someone considering homosexuality unnatural and detrimental, we label everyone intolerant and work harder to make white people more inclusive: less moral.

Being individuals, we have no interest in a family, race, or other body politic suffering harm because an individual harms himself or herself. We are supposed to tolerate other people's perversions and self-destruction because they supposedly do us personally no harm.

The only harm about which we care is harm to each of us personally. That harm might be to no more than our feelings, but that is enough. So consumed are we with people's beliefs in this Age of Ideology, any dissent becomes harmful, however private or ancient the dissent. We refuse to tolerate other people's morality or viewpoints different to ours because our feelings of offence are the worst harm we can sense.

Ours is an ideology called tolerance, ordaining what others must tolerate. Demanding tolerance only makes us intolerant of anything else. Our new totalitarianism demands our compatriots be as tolerant as we are. We impose our tolerance.

Ideologies of inclusion are as much the exclusion of our race, families, and culture. We are inclusive, but not of people who are not inclusive as we are: them, we exclude. Ideologies of inclusion for all ultimately amount to exclusion of some.

Diversity does not extend to dissenting views; diversity without dissent. Ideologies of diversity shut down diversity of thought, especially but not only as regards matters of race, gender, and sexuality.

As we do with other discriminations we dislike, we do not just ban discrimination against so-called transgenderism and homosexuality. We demonise the discriminators.

Two plus two equals five because powerful people say it does. Only bigots disagree.

Diversity reflects Western individualism. Released from reality and rejecting any social or biological norms, people desperate to be different to the people around them become ever nuttier, weirder and more depraved than the nutty, weird, and depraved people around them. Never does the sameness of diversity become more grotesque.

The West's only deviants are ideological. There is no sexual desire so perverse for which we will call someone a deviant, but we will jump to call a normal person a bigot.

Trying to satisfy our tribal instincts, the mob shouting down racists also shouts down moralists. Only in the tribeless West is being called a morals campaigner considered an insult.

Ideological tribalism is set upon biological tribalism. It is set upon us.

Gender ideology is fantasy, but in this Age of Ideology, telling the truth about race, gender, and sexuality is dissent. The mob shouts down gender realists no less than it shouts down racial realists.

Facts and certainty are unethical. Lies are ethical.

Ideologues demand lies and immorality, leaving people alone. Instead of homosexuality and other aberrant behaviours being a crime, telling the truth about human biology or expressing morality became much like a crime. Caring loud enough about others to want them to recover their heterosexual nature or be comfortable with their biological gender so explicitly as to be called vilification often is a crime.

In our Age of Ideology, we dictate people's beliefs, but not facts. We tell people what to believe about gender and sexuality, but reject gender as a biological fact and heterosexuality as our biological norm. We tell people what to think, but not what they are.

Mental Illness

Mental illness being among our new political constructs, homosexuality is no longer the mental illness so alien. Instead, so obvious to us has homosexuality being normal suddenly become, the mental illness is not embracing homosexuality as part of a supposed diversity of life, but not diversity of opinion.

That illness we call homophobia. A minority knows it has arrived in our tribeless West when there is a postmodern phobia in its defence.

Human nature is not just racist and sexist. It is homophobic.

Estranged as we are from human nature, we cannot comprehend a person engaged with human nature. Being individuals, we cannot comprehend tribalism. We cannot imagine anyone caring enough about others of their race to see something sad in homosexuality harming homosexuals, their families, and the race they share.

We thus presume the person fears homosexuals or homosexuality. The fear might be of their race and family dying, but homophobia deems it irrational, as if reason commands that we disregard our race and families.

We particularly like to explain homophobia in our Freudian West by claiming homophobes are repressing their homosexual desires. It is an incontrovertible claim no amount of denial can refute. People can hardly be aware of desires they are supposedly repressing.

What applies to homosexuality applies to transgenderism. Any suggestion that so-called transgendered men or women are not really men or women is deemed transphobic, for insisting the transgendered do not magically become their new gender. Anatomical reality does not come into it.

More often than not, we simply cite phobias as a means of abuse. Lambasting a person for being homophobic, transphobic, this-phobic, or that-phobic does not require rationale.

In the name of inclusion, any reluctance by white people to embrace everyone is one phobia or another, except one. We do not embrace ourselves: our families and race.

We embrace people of other religions and homosexuals feeling marginalised, but not Christians and other moralists. More mental illness as a political construct, morality and Christianity are becoming mental illnesses in the tribeless West for affecting people's dealings with others. Anything but complete individualism, in submission to our new Western orthodoxies, becomes mental illness. Tribalism becomes mental illness.

Other religions can keep their moralities. Only Christians must be individuals.

Even while lecturing other races to tolerate homosexuality and so-called transgenderism, we do not like to abuse them for being homophobic or transphobic. We do not abuse them at all.

Homosexuals and the so-called transgendered of colour might call those of their race homophobic or transphobic, especially when living in the West. We do not. We only abuse white people.

Instead of equality, there has become homosexual privilege, even homosexual superiority. We make no provision for people discovering or rediscovering their heterosexuality, as we make for them supposedly discovering their homosexuality.

Counsellors and other medical health professionals lose their right to decide what is in their patients' best interests, when it comes to homosexuality and so-called transgenderism. So do patients.

Our suicidal ethics prevent counsellors from telling the truth about gender and sexuality, even to patients who want to hear truth. We are banning therapies curing people of homosexual urges, even for people who want to be cured.

Denying homosexuals the freedom to be cured of whatever longings or traumas lead them to homosexual desires is oppressive. For all our rejection of paternalism, we insist that homosexuals should not want to be well.

Commercial Interests

Western businesses embrace sexual and gender diversity for much the same reason they embrace racial diversity: money. Without being races to think of the future, Western capitalism wants homosexuality. They are both excesses of our individualism, underpinned by the same immorality and other indifference to people's well-being.

Long-term cohabitants need not make homosexuals less solitary. Even more than homosexuals, the most committed of employees and most solitary of people are asexual. Solitariness and childlessness allow employees to remain completely committed to their careers.

Without thoughts of the future, homosexuals save less money than heterosexual people do. They spend.

The only thing we like more than homosexuality is business. Selling products, we promote individualism: disconnectedness. We will portray pretty well anything when there is money to be made: men eschewing relationships with women to the point of letting them die; happy homosexuals. We deem vice a virtue and virtue a vice, pretending pain is pleasure and pleasure is pain, for the sake of more profit.

Homosexuality does not just define Western homosexuals. Like the rest of our rejection of biological difference and relationship, our absolute individualism, it defines our tribeless West.

Other races earning money by catering to Western and Jewish homosexuals are being opportunistic. In a world of racial identities, they typically treat homosexual white people as being white rather than homosexual, much as they treat white women foremost as being white. A homosexual with money is money.

Never are we a more grotesque, money-hungry moral vacuum than we are when we promote homosexuality among our race for the income it brings. A woman selling her sexual services, we call a prostitute. The West doing so, we call diversity.

Homosexual Imperialism

We once reached out from Europe to spread civilisation across the earth, as no other race has done. Romantic love was a Western idea we shared with the world, when we knew romance could only be between a man and a woman.

If people are born homosexual and if race is merely a social construct, then homosexuality should be equally prevalent across all races, but we have become more likely than people from other races to be homosexual. Jews appear always to have been more likely than people from other races to be homosexual. Homosexuals among other races are a relative rarity, although we seize upon those rarities to blind us to how different we are.

Where homosexuality goes, so does transgenderism. Jews also appear to be more likely than people of other races to be so-called transgendered. They pioneered transgenderism.

White people are the only races to reject their races, countries, and cultures. We have given up our empires of civilisation.

Our only chore remaining is imposing upon others our new rules of what to do, although we do not realise we are imposing because we think all races are the same. The West's refusal to assert our past sciences, religion, and other cultures does not keep us from asserting our post-scientific, post-religious, and other post-cultural ideologies.

We impose our deepest demands upon white people. Our ideologies of isolation related to race we keep to ourselves, but we try to impose our rejection of biological gender and the instincts that gender engender upon the rest of the world.

Donning our plastic laurels, our mission is sexual and gender individualism. The human rights we promote are to homosexuality and transgenderism, not to living by human natures in accord with our natural desires and fulfilment. We espouse freedom but not freedom to live by our evolutionary psychology.

Our new-found horror at our past European imperialism seeking to spread civilisation does not deter us from a new Western imperialism seeking to spread sexual immorality. Rich and powerful people want someone to pleasure them. We who once spread civilisation now spread sodomy.

We might have long done so. Peoples had no need to prohibit behaviour other than men lying with women when nobody contemplated anything else. Tribes and races that had never contemplated homosexuality did so after Christian missionaries quoted the Bible's clear condemnation of it.

For the Bible to need to be clear, homosexuality must have been a problem in the Middle East when Biblical texts were being written. Jews might have introduced homosexuality to Europe.

The empires we now try to craft do not call Christianity our faith. We are atheistic imperialists, but imperialists no less.

Foisting corruptions of nature upon others, our postmodern empires of individualism do not depend upon force. We lecture and bribe. The journalism, entertainment, and other media that have been so effective at changing public opinion in the West seek the same influence elsewhere.

We are having some success, compromising countries closest to the West, at least among those people for whom closeness to the West is useful to them. The West so keen to apologise for our honourable imperial past now has a dishonourable imperial present for which we can come in time to apologise, if we ever right ourselves again.

Whether by law or merely by mores, most of the world continues to reject homosexuality for being unnatural and harming families and society, as we did until recently. Races other than ours retain more human nature we once knew better than we know it now. They retain their racial identities and communities so do not need sexual identities and communities. They retain their religious conviction. There is more to their lives than money. They make laws of morality.

Being of different races, they generally do not care what we do among ourselves. They might even welcome our decline.

Polygamy

If any parents in British schools are able to protect their children from indoctrination with Jewish and now Western attitudes to gender and sexuality, they are Muslim parents. They defend and assert their cultures as we no longer defend or assert ours, and there are a lot of them. If the West's worsening absurdity and depravity around gender and sexuality makes the coming of sharia appear a little less horrifying, then perhaps that is the idea.

The tribeless West promotes homosexuality less to Muslim children than to white children, but we do not ban homosexuality so as not to offend people of other religions as we ban Christmas and Easter. Our vision for a single world civilisation includes homosexuality. It does not include carols.

While the tribeless West allows marriages that minimise procreation, Muslims pursue marriages that maximise it. For all our talk of diversity, equality, and inclusion, no Western countries recognise polygamy, not even among homosexuals.

Homosexuality is plainly unnatural. Polygamy might be natural.

Polygamy is serial heterosexuality. Some animal species are monogamous while others are not, probably because of the practicalities of bearing and raising offspring. Primates are more likely to be monogamous than other mammals, but something like sixty percent of primitive human societies allowed polygamy. We would fare better with polygamous commitment than monogamous individualism.

Genocide

When Noah accepted two of every species of animal onto his ark, he took a male and a female. They were not simply male and female identified, or the species would have perished with the flood.

Eradicating gender eradicates sexuality. Eradicating sexuality eradicates procreation.

Emboldened by every success, ideologies have become more and more extreme, through dogma more and more destructive. Sexual organs become remnant, dismissing any significance for sperm, ovaries, or a womb.

Transgenderism is a rejection of procreation, with or without surgery or sterilisation, even if some of the so-called transgendered retain their natural instinct to procreate. When the so-called transgendered are sterilised, then transgenderism may be the cruellest hoax ever imposed upon vulnerable people. If it all reduces the likelihood of people marrying and bearing children, then the tribeless West thinks that is desirable.

Homosexuality and every other sexuality incapable of bearing children are nihilistic sexualities: suited to people without faith in the future. The philosophical foundation of gender ideology is nihilism more than Marxism. Without childbearing, there is no future.

Whatever else people might think of sexuality or gender, no person caring for the future of a family or race could want to promote a lifestyle that diminishes the chances of new generations being born, when that family and race are in rapid decline. He or she could only want to discourage the nonsense about race, gender, and sexuality increasingly espoused around the West of late, or anything else that reduces a family and race's reproduction.

Tribespeople aid and defend homosexuals and the gender dysphoric from among their tribe, provided they are not harming other tribespeople. They do not promote or defend homosexuality or gender dysphoria.

People are not coerced into homosexuality as much as coaxed into it, but it is hard to think of anything crueller to do to a person, his family and forebears, her children never born, and their people than to promote sexual diversity. If homosexuality is sexual suicide, then legitimising homosexuality is sexual homicide.

Discouraging or preventing procreation pushes a family, clan, and race towards extinction. Eradicating procreation eradicates a family, clan, and race.

Ideologies around race and gender are so plainly irrational and destructive, the most reasonable explanation for their imposition across the West is hostility to the point of genocide. If it is not another race loathing us, then it is those of our race loathing our own. If any person promoting gender ideology is not hostile to the West, then he or she is horribly indifferent.

Whatever the polyglot of thoughts inside people's heads, any lifestyle to the exclusion of bearing children can hardly be in a person, family, or race's interests when that family and race are dying. Whether transgenderism or homosexuality is any more or less unnatural than deliberate childlessness is of little consequence. They all defy human nature. They all lack human fulfilment.

Individuals, families, and races might well be better served by gender-dysphoric and homosexual people bearing children than mentally healthy heterosexuals not bearing children. If putting aside their gender dysphoria and homosexual feelings to produce children makes them seem heroic, then perhaps they are.

A Right to Die

Our ancestors struggled against winters, famine, floods, and conflict. Other races still do. We are no longer so stoic or heroic.

Not just venerating each individual but also the families and societies who suffer when one among them dies, Western Civilisation prohibited suicide. Life is precious.

Slowly, we are surrendering, relaxing that prohibition. Rejecting paternalism means demanding a right to self-harm: drugs, self-mutilation, suicide.

Self-harm used to be immoral because we harmed not just our individual selves, but also our family, race, and world at large. The tribeless West accepts self-harm because we feel no connection with our family, race, or world. If we do not want the harm, then we do not do the act.

The narrowest of senseless self-interest and ultimate expression of our self-absorption, self-indulgence, and living for the instant, is suicide. It is the pinnacle of victimless crimes, for people certain we are simply individuals without stakes in each other's lives. While Japanese see suicide as a means of honouring their families and race, Western individualism allows us to kill ourselves for whatever reason we want.

Pain is easier to bear when we know the curse is temporary, especially when redress is within our control. Loneliness, shame, and poverty are not reasons to die unless rationally or irrationally we feel they are interminable and insurmountable.

Old people sharing their memories of good and bad experiences offer more than advice. Theirs are the comforting perspectives of people who have survived their problems, assuring younger people they too will in time recover from their problems. However bad the pain of a broken relationship, the collapse of a career, or the death of someone close might feel, lives do get better. Hard times pass.

When the cause of our pain is a terminal disease, then wanting to die is not just giving up without a fight. It is giving up on the rest of us finding a cure. We do not believe in us anymore.

Our glib acceptance that dying can be better than staying alive affirms our Western suicide: the logical culmination, conclusion, to our estrangement from human nature, reality, and love. Death with dignity is still death, with much less dignity than fighting honourably to live.

We have lost our natural instinct to survive, collectively and individually. What remains is an unnatural instinct to die.

Empathy, community, and morality have gone so our people will go too. We live and let others live and die. Men and women willing to die get what they want.

They are the most tragic of the dying. Someone left to care will miss them more than they would have missed themselves.

Old men and women die, but families and a people endure while ever new generations replace them, living the most fulfilling lives they can. When a generation dies childless, generational suicide, a family dies too. When all families die, a race dies too: mere footnotes in the stories of other people's lives. The indefeasibility of the individual is the demise of a quickly shrinking group: suicide Europe, the suicidal West.

We to whom individualism is paramount are killing the politic within us. Without societies there can be no social suicide, but we are the body suicide. It is finally each individual's demise.

Sometime, surely, it can stop. We are the kings and queens of ideologies to make everything all right, but we would not be dying if everything were fine.

If homosexuality is the despair of being abandoned, then Western individualism leaves us all in despair. Restoring our racial identities, no longer would we need gender identities and suffer so fractious a division between men and women. Re-engaging with biological reality, so-called transgenderism and the rest of gender ideology falls away.

Recovering our biological loyalties, respecting our tribal instincts, our other natural instincts should revive. Aberrant sexualities should diminish. The trials of life are easier to bear with families and races on which we can rely.

CONCLUSION

If we are not to be solitary individuals disappearing in a lonely great seethe of people, then we have to be biological tribes: families, clans, and races. Feeling kinship with our race wherever we are can be comforting for white people as it is for everyone else. Founding our identity upon race gives us something to share with the rest of our race around the world. Losing our racial identities has not given us anything to share with people of another race living across the street.

Race is our only real means for identity: the only tangible collective identity wider than family, and we need something wider than family if our families are not to fade away or fall in among themselves. Races are substantive, grounded in fact, set before we were born and unchanging: our forebears' shared descendants.

Identities by birth endure. Other identities do not.

We assume race only ever divides people, but we have become the most divided peoples on earth: divided by work, wealth, and values, class and age, gender and sexuality. They define and divide us because we lost what once defined and united us. They became more important than they needed to be.

Racial belonging could breach the social, political, and economic divisions between us, the discriminations and prejudices. It does for all other races.

It is not so much racial unification, because we used to be more united than we are now. It is racial reunification. Racial unity can overcome our differences, instead of our differences (most obviously our different views about race) driving us further apart.

Racism, nationalism, and other tribalism connect people together. Without them, white people are the most solitary people on earth.

ABOUT THE AUTHOR

Simon Lennon has travelled throughout Europe, America, Australasia, Asia, and the South Pacific, seeing how similar European peoples are to each other (wherever we live) and how different we of the West are to everyone else. He has university bachelor's degrees in science and law and university master's degrees in commerce and business. He is married with six children.

His non-fiction collection *The West* comprises the following sixteen books:

Mending the West
The Unnatural West: An Overview
The Tribeless West: An Overview
The Homeless West: An Overview
The Vanishing West: An Overview

Individualism
Western Individualism
The End of Natural Selection
The Need for Nations

Identity
People's Identity: Race and Racism
Of Whom We're Born: Race and Family
Biological Us: Gender and Sexuality

Nationalism
A Land to Belong: Nationalism
The Failure of Multiculturalism

Cultures
Reclaiming Western Cultures
Christendom Lost
Aiding Islam

He is also the author of another non-fiction book, two collections of short stories, and five novels.

www.ingramcontent.com/pod-product-compliance
Lightning Source LLC
Chambersburg PA
CBHW021619270326
41931CB00008B/770